Learn Java and
Master Writing Code

- A step-by-step guide from a beginner to a Java programmer

- More than 100 Java code exercises, including all of the answers at the end of this book.

- Download the source code and learn fast by practicing and doing

- Learn to read Java code, understand it, change it and test it to see the results.

- Write your own Java-code.

- Learn the basic concept of object-oriented programming

- Prior experience in coding is not required in order to start this book

Sar Maroof

Table of Contents

Introduction

This book is organized to teach Java to beginners, and it guides readers to master writing code by working with more than 100 examples, exercises, and assignments.

Prior experience in coding is not required in order to start this book. It explains Java in an easy to understand way, with simple coding examples and many exercises that make it interesting and helpful to the reader even if they have no prior experience in programming.

It is difficult for any expert software developer to believe that anyone can learn to program by only reading books. All experts build their experiences by doing and practicing programming. That is the exact reason why this book focuses also on working with a complete code that is specially designed for anyone who wants to learn Java.

You can download the source code for this book on the website of the author, **www.sarmaroof.com**, and follow the guide to set up the code in a Java development environment.

Once you establish the code, you can start to enjoy working with it and writing your own code by executing the exercises and the tasks of the book. By clicking on one button, you can compile and run each code and see the effect that your code has.

Sar Maroof is a professional software development teacher. He publishes technical articles and has also worked for more than a decade in developing software for large, as well as small companies, and also as a freelancer.

Sar Maroof

Is This Book for You?

If you ask the question whether this book is for you, the answer is to look at the following simple Java code, which is a simple class that describes cars. If you don't understand a single line of the following code, you are a real beginner. Don' t worry because this book assumes that you are a beginner. It starts at the very beginning of understanding programming. By following the chapters you will gradually learn standard Java, understand it and start writing your own code.

If you understand the following code completely and you have some experiences with programming, this book will help you to improve your Java skills.

I would recommend beginners to start from the beginning and read the "Basic Knowledge".

Example 1

```java
class Car
{
    String brand;
    int mileage;
    double price;

    public static void main(String[] args)
    {
        Car car1 = new Car();
        car1.brand = "Nissan";
        car1.mileage = 7000;
        car1.price = 6500.25;

        System.out.print( car1.brand + ", ");
        System.out.print( car1.price + ", ");
        System.out.print( car1.mileage);
    }
}
```

Basic Knowledge

This book focuses on learning programming by reading the explanation and practicing with programming code. That is far more interesting and easier to learn than only reading the theoretical explanation. I would strongly recommend to download the source code of this book on my website and follow the step by step explanation of how to install JSE (Java Standard Edition). Notice that some versions of Java are called JDK (Java Development Kit). You can find on the previously mentioned website the explanation of how to set up the source code of this book in an IDE (Integrated Development Environment). Start to read the following Basic Knowledge so that you understand how programming works and what kinds of tools and software you need to compile and run a Java code.

1. Java Editor Ide (Integrated Development Environment)

We use as a Java editor, Eclipse including JSE (Java Standard Editon), which are both free to download. Java is a platform-independent programming language, which is why you can run Java programs on every operating system.

2. Compiling And Running Programs

Many beginners might scare to hear "compiling and running a program", but in fact, you can do that by clicking on the green button, see arrow one in the picture below. By compiling and running the following program "Nissan, 6500.25, 7000" is written to the standard output, see arrow two in the picture below. Compiling is the translation of source code into machine language with the help of a tool called a compiler. After compiling a source code, the program is directly executable.

The picture below shows how Eclipse IDE looks like, which we use to edit Java programs. The arrow two points to the standard output of the program. When you compile and run the program, you see the output in that part of the screen.

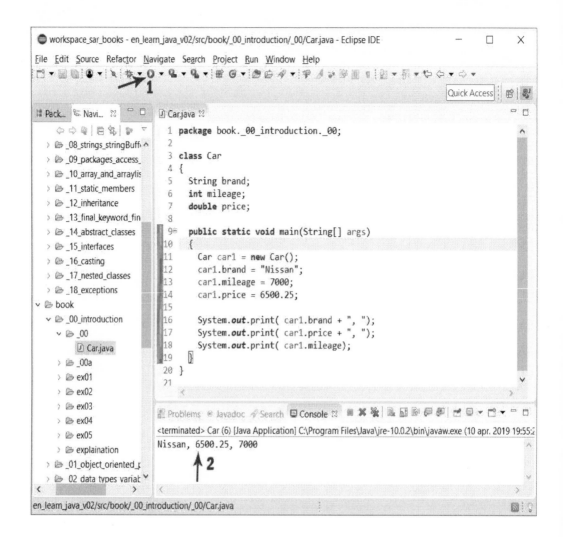

3. Java Classes And Interfaces

Java programs are mostly classes and interfaces. These two concepts are covered in details later in this book. For now, you need only to learn that a class in Java begins with a statement as **class Person**. Person is the name of the class, that can be chosen by programmers. Every class in Java is stored in a file with the name of the class and the extension of **.java**. The class Person should be stored in a file called **Person.java**. Each class name begins with the keyword class, and each interface name begins with the keyword interface. Classes and interfaces also have members like variables and methods. Methods are blocks, which are written between curly braces.

Example 2
The following is a class that describes products and is stored in a file with the name Product.java

```
class Product
{
  // code
}
```

The following interface must also be stored in a file with the name Payable.java.

Example 3
```
interface Payable
{
  // code
}
```

4. Statements

Statements in Java are similar to sentences in natural languages and are executable units. A statement usually ends with a semicolon (;).

Examples of statements are:

```
String name = "Emily";
int age = 22;
```

5. Code Block

The code in Java is within a start and an end brace, and it is called a block of code. Below are some examples of block codes.

Block type	Block style
| Class | ```java
class Computer
{
    // code
}
``` |
| Method | ```java
void setBrand()
{
    // code
}
```
The keyword void means that the method doesn't return any values. |
| Conditional statements | ```java
if(age < 18)
{
    discount = %10;
}
``` |
| Iteration | ```java
for( int i=0; i<5; i ++)
{
    // code
}
``` |

6. The Main Method

The main method is a method that is needed to execute a Java program. The main method begins with **public static void main(String[] args)** and is followed by a block code as shown below.

```java
public static void main(String[] args)
{
    // code
}
```

For the moment it is important to learn the following about the main method.

- All executable programs must have a main method such as the code below.
- The statements within the block of the main method are executed.
- The execution of the statements inside the main method block is done from top to bottom.
- In the next example, **statement 1** is first executed, then **statement 2,** and at last
- **statement 3**.
- The following code writes **253** to the standard output.

Example 4

```java
class Calculator
{
  // statements;
  // main method
  public static void main(String[] args)
  {
    System.out.print(2); // statement 1;
    System.out.print(5); // statement 2;
    System.out.print(3); // statement 3;
  }
}
```

7. Writing Values Of Variables And Texts To The Standard Output

The statement **System.out.println();** is used to write values of variables and texts to the standard output and it is a practical way to test the output of your program. It is not necessary for now to understand all the details about this statement, but it is important to know that you can use it to test the output of your programs.

If you compile and run the next code, the following is written to the standard output:

Ronald

35

My name is Emma.

Age: 35 year

Example 5

```java
class Doctor
{
  public static void main(String[] args)
  {
    String name = "Ronald";  // variable name is a String type
    int age = 35; // Variable age is an integer type

    // statement 1 writes the value of name
    // to the standard output
    System.out.println(name);
    // statement 2 writes the value of age
    // to the standard output
    System.out.println(age);
    // statement 3 writes the text "My name is Emma."
    // to the standard output
    System.out.println("My name is Emma.");
    /*
     *  statement 4 writes a combination of a text and
     *  a value of a variable to the standard output
     */
    System.out.println("Age: " + age + " year");
```

```
    }
}
```

To write a text to the standard output, it must be between quotation marks, but for the values of variables that are not required, see the **statements 1, 2 and 3** in the previous example.

To write a combination of texts and values of variables to the standard output, you need to use the plus (+) sign between the variable name and the text, see **statement 4** in the previous example. To write the texts and the variables on one line to the standard output you need to use **System.out.print** instead of **System.out.println.**

8. Comments

Comments are ignored by the compiler. Below are two ways to add comments to your code.

1. Comment of a single line begins with two slashes //.
    Everything on the right side of these characters, see Java as comments:

    ```
    // comment of a single-line
    ```

2. Comment of multiple lines starts with /* and ends with */.
    Everything between these two characters sees Java as comments:

    ```
    /*
      here is a comment
      of multiple lines
    */
    ```

9. The Keyword Public

Java supports controlling access to the classes and class members by using special keywords. Using the **public** keyword before the keyword **class** or the class members (variables and methods) indicates that the class or the member is accessible from other classes. This will be covered in this book later in details.

Important to Know

1 Java Standard API (Application Programming Interface)

Java provides a lot of code that can be reused by programmers. It is important for every Java programmer to use this free rich library, which is why it is introduced in this book. For some of the assignments, you need to open this document which helps with how to use the code. You can find the Java standard API documentation on the website of Oracle.

2 Escape Sequences

An escape sequence is a character preceded by a backslash. These characters have a special meaning for the compiler. For example, if you have a double quote within a double quote, you must use escape sequences, see the following example. If you need to write the text "He says: "I go to London."" to the standard output, you should do that as follows.

```
System.out.print("He says: \"I go to London\".");
```

Example 6

```
class Symbol
{
  public static void main(String[] args)
  {
    System.out.println("Apostrophe      : " + "abcde\'fghij");
    System.out.println("Quotation mark : " + "abcde\"fghij");
    System.out.println("Backslash       : " + "abcde\\fghij");
    System.out.println("New line        : " + "abcde\nfghij");
    System.out.println("New line 2      : " + "abcde\ffghij");
    System.out.println("Tab             : " + "abcde\tfghij");
    System.out.print("It was written \"Parking is not Allowed.\".");
  }
}
```

If you compile and run the above code, the following is written to the standard output.

```
Apostrophe      : abcde'fghij

Quotation mark : abcde"fghij

Backslash       : abcde\fghij

New line        : abcde

fghij

New line 2      : abcde_fghij

Tab             : abcde    fghij
```

It was written "Parking is not Allowed.".

The table of the escape sequences:

Escape sequence	Description
\'	single quote
\"	double quote
\\	backslash character
\b	backspace
\n	Newline
\r	carriage return
\t	Tab
\f	form feed

1. Object Oriented Programming

Java is an object-oriented programming language. The OO techniques allow you to build computer programs using objects that interact and communicate with each other.

Each object contains variables and methods through which they work together. Java sees everything as an object so, people, animals, plants, and things around you are treated as objects.

Example of objects are: **student, employee, customer, company, chair, laptop, mobile, animal, plant** and so on.

To create an object, you need first to create a template or a description of the object, and that is called a **class**. Below is explained how to create a Java class. Once you create a class you can instantiate unlimited numbers of objects from it.

To make it clear how Java deals with classes, we use the following example. Suppose you are asked to write a small program for an employer who saves the names, ages, and salaries of his employees. The name, age, and salary are called the **attributes** or the **variables** of the class.

To write this simple program, we have to take the next steps.

1.1. Creating A Class Employee

- As has already been explained in this book, each Java class is stored in a file with the name of the class and the extension **.Java**. In this case, we store the class Employee in the file **Employee.Java**.

- A class starts with the Java keyword class followed by the name of the class and a block of code as shown in the next example:

The employer wants to keep the **names, ages,** and **salari**es of his employees. Within the class **Employee**, we declare variables for these three attributes.

Each attribute starts with a data type or variable type (more details about data types will be covered later in this book. In this example, we use the following three data types.

Data types	Used for
String	The string type is used in Java for a combination of symbols, numbers and letters such as names and texts.
int	The int type is used for integers such as ages.
double	The double type is used for decimal numbers such as prices and salaries.

Example 1
```
class Employee
{
    // the attributes (variables) of the class
```

```
String name;
int age;
double salary;

// the main method to execute the code
public static void main(String[] args)
{
   // more code
}
}
```

So far we have created the class Employee, we can create as many employee objects as we want.

1.2. Creating Objects Based On The Class Employee

- In order to execute the Employee class, the main method should be defined as it is already explained in this book.

  □ We can create as many employee objects as we need. As examples, we make two objects for the employees Emma and Jack.

  □ An object has a name and you may choose any name you wish for the objects you create.

  □ In the following example, we create the object **employee1** for Emma and the object **em-ployee2** for Jack. Remember that Emma and Jack are the names of the two employee objects. The object in our example contains the names, the ages and the salaries of Emma and Jack.

  □ In Java we can create an object by first writing the name of the class then the name of the object follows by the equal sign and the Java keyword **new** then the name of the class and ends by open and closed parentheses. At last, a semicolon as shown below.

```
// create object employee1
Employee employee1 = new Employee();
```

Notice: Java class names start always with capital letters, while the names of objects and attributes start with small letters.

Example 2
```
class Employee
{
   // the attributes (variables) of the class
   String name;
   int age;
   double salary;

   // the main method to execute the code
   public static void main(String[] args)
   {
      // create object employee1
```

```
        Employee employee1 = new Employee();
        // create object employee2
        Employee employee2 = new Employee();
    }
}
```

1.3. Assigning Values To The Variables

To assign values to the variables, we use the name of the object separated from the variable name by a dot (.) then the equal sign and at last the value of the variable.

The following statements assign the values "Emma, 24, 2500.55" respectively to the variables name, age, and salary of the object employee1.

Note: the value of a string should be between quotes as shown below.

```
employee1.name = "Emma";
employee1.age = 24;
employee1.salary = 2500.55;
```

The following code doesn't contain errors, but nothing will be visible if you compile and run it. The reason is that we only told the computer to memorize the names, ages, and salaries of two employee objects namely Emma and Jack. That is comparable with human's memory when you memorize the multiplication tables, for example, you know that 6 x 5 is equal to 30, but you give the answer only when someone asks you or you need it.

Example 3
```
class Employee
{
    String name;
    int age;
    double salary;

    public static void main(String[] args)
    {
        // create object employee1
        Employee employee1 = new Employee();
        /*
         *  assign values to the
         *  variables of the object employee1
         */
        employee1.name = "Emma";
        employee1.age = 24;
        employee1.salary = 2500.55;

        // create object employee2
        Employee employee2 = new Employee();
        /* assign values to the
         * variables of the object employee2
         */
        employee2.name = "Jack";
        employee2.age = 32;
        employee2.salary = 2800.45;
```

```
    }
}
```

1.4. Accessing The Attribute's Values Of The Objects

To access the variables of the objects, you can use the name of the object and the variable name separated by a dot "." as shown below. In this step, we try to ask the program to write the data of the objects " employee1 and employee2" to the standard output. It is obvious that everyone can memorize the data of two employees of our example, but the power of the computer is that it can memorize almost unlimited data of unlimited objects and that is beyond the capability of humans. In the following examples, we ask the program to show the data that we programmed as explained before in this book by using the following statement.

```java
System.out.print(employee1.name + ", ");
```

If the next program is compiled and run, the following is written to the standard output.

```
Emma, 24, 2400.55
Jack, 32, 2800.45
```

Example 4

```java
class Employee
{
    String name;
    int age;
    double salary;

    public static void main(String[] args)
    {
        // create object employee1
        Employee employee1 = new Employee();
        /* assign values to the
         * variables of the object employee1
         */
        employee1.name = "Emma";
        employee1.age = 24;
        employee1.salary = 2400.55;

        // create object employee2
        Employee employee2 = new Employee();
        /* assign values to the
         * variables of the object employee2
         */
        employee2.name = "Jack";
        employee2.age = 32;
        employee2.salary = 2800.45;
```

```
        // print employee data;
        System.out.print(employee1.name + ", ");
        System.out.print(employee1.age+ ", " );
        System.out.println(employee1.salary);
        System.out.print(employee2.name + ", ");
        System.out.print(employee2.age+ ", " );
        System.out.println(employee2.salary);
    }
}
```

There are some important principles of object-oriented programming such as Inheritance, and Encapsulation. In the following chapters, you will find more explanation of object-oriented programming using Java code. Remember that this book is about learning Java as a programming language, but offers only some basic principles of object-oriented programming.

1.5. Inheritance

Inheritance is one of the important principles of object-oriented programming. The concept of Inheritance supports reusability of code that has already been written. To reuse the existing code you create parent and child classes. The parent classes are called super classes and a child class, which extends the code of the superclass is called a subclass. You can find more details about inheritance and how it works with code examples in the chapter Inheritance.

1.6. Polymorphism

This is the possibility of using a single method name for multiple methods by applying specific rules. There are two types of polymorphism, which are explained below.

- **Overriding methods**

By applying this technique you can override the superclass methods in the subclass. The subclass method has the same name, the same type and the same number of arguments as the superclass.

- **Overloading methods**

In the case of overloading, the methods also have the same name, but they have different types and/or different number of arguments.

You can find more details about overriding and overloading methods in the chapter Inheritance.

1.7. Encapsulation

This concerns the possibility of concealing data by limiting the direct access to the variables, but instead of that using the public accessors and mutators. Accessories are used to provide information about the status of an object, while you can use mutators for changing the status of an object. Accessors in Java starts with the word get, while mutators start with the word set. They are also called getters and setters. In the chapter Methods, Package and access modifiers, you will learn more about methods and accesses.

Quiz 1: Objects of the Class Car

What happens when the following program is compiled and run?

```java
class Car
{
  String brand;
  int mileage;
  double price;

  public static void main(String[] args)
  {
    Car car1 = new Car();
    Car car2 = new Car();
    Car car3 = new Car();

    car1.brand = "Volkswagen";
    car1.mileage = 4000;
    car1.price = 4500.75;
    car2.brand = "Mazda";
    car2.mileage = 2000;
    car2.price = 3500.65;
    car3.brand = "Nissan";
    car3.mileage = 7000;
    car3.price = 6500.25;

    System.out.print(car2.brand + ", ");
    System.out.print(car3.price + ", ");
    System.out.print(car1.mileage);
  }
}
```

Select the correct answer.
- a) This code writes Volkswagen, 4500.75, 4000 to standard output.
- b) This code writes Mazda, 3500.65, 2000 to standard output.
- c) This code writes Mazda, 6500.25, 4000 to standard output.
- d) This code writes Volkswagen, 3500.65, 4000 to standard output.
- e) This code writes Nissan, 3500.65, 4000 to the standard output.

Explanation
car2.brand writes Mazda to the standard output, because the statement car2.brand = "Mazda"; assigns the value Mazda to the variable brand of car2.
car3.price writes 6500.25 to the standard output, because the statement car3.price = 6500.25; assigns the value 6500.25 to the variable price.
car1.mileage writes 4000 to the standard output, because the statement
car1.mileage = 4000; assigns the value of 4000 to the variable mileage of car 1.

The correct answer is: c.

Exercises

For all of the car objects, you want to add the color of the car. Assume that the color of the object car1 is black, of car2 is red and car3 is white.

Update the class Car so that the following should be written to the standard output if the code is compiled and run.

Brand 1: Volkswagen, color: black

Brand 2: Mazda, color: red

Brand 3: Nissan, color: white

Quiz 2: Objects of the Class Animal

What happens when the following code is compiled and run?

```java
class Animal
{
  String name;
  String sort = "pet";

  public static void main(String[] args)
  {
    Animal animal1 = new Animal();
    Animal animal2 = new Animal();
    Animal animal3 = new Animal();

    animal1.name = "Tiger";
    animal1.sort = "predator";
    animal2.name = "Dog";
    animal3.name = "cow";

    System.out.print(animal1.name +", "+animal3.sort);
  }
}
```

Select the correct answer.
   a)   This code writes Tiger, pet to the standard output.
   b)   This code writes Tiger, predator to the standard export.
   c)   This code writes cow, predator to the standard export.
   d)   This code writes Dog, pet to the standard output.

Explanation

The first part of the statement System.out.print (animal1.name +", "+animal3.sort); is "animal1.name".
The statement animal1.name = "Tiger"; assigns the value Tiger to the name of the object animal1.

The initial value of sort is pet. If there is no value assigned with the variable sort the initial value remains the value of the variable sort, which is pet. That is why the second part of "animal3.sort" writes the sort pet for the animal3 object to the standard output.

The correct answer is: a.

Exercises

The above code does not work as desired. Improve the code so that the following is written to the standard output by compiling and running the code.

Animal 1: Tiger, Sort: predator
Animal 2: Dog, Sort: pet
Animal 3: cow, Sort: farm animal

Quiz 3: The Number of Objects of the Class Computer

How many computer objects are created in the next program?

```java
class Computer
{
  String brand;
  int hardDisk;
  int ram;

  public static void main(String[] args)
  {
    Computer comp = new Computer();
    Computer myComputer = new Computer();
    Computer aComputer = new Computer();
    Computer computer = new Computer();
  }
}
```

Select the correct answer.
   a) This code does not create any computer objects.
   b) This code creates three computer objects.
   c) This code creates four computer objects.
   d) This code creates five computer objects.
   e) This code creates two computer objects.

Explanation

There are four statements in this program that create objects using the Java keyword new. Those statements create the objects comp, myComputer, aComputer and computer. So, there are four computer objects created.

The correct answer is: c.

Exercises

Assign the values HP, 500 and 8 respectively to the variables brand, hard disk, and ram of the object myComputer. By compiling and running the program, the following should be written to the standard output.

Brand: HP
Hard disk: 120 GB
RAM: 8 GB

2. Data Types & Variables

2.1 What are variables?

A variable is a memory location, which could be used to store a value. Variables have names that are chosen by programmers. A variable should be declared before using it and its value can be changed.

There are 8 primitive data types (variables) in Java. Those types are: **byte, short, int, long, float, double, char and boolean,** which are divided into 4 categories as shown below.

Data Type (bits)	Range, Description and Examples
Integer Type	
byte (8 bits)	-2^7 to $2^7 - 1$, -128 to 127 The byte type is small and can be used to save memory. Its default value is 0. **Example: byte b = 20;**
short (16 bits)	-2^{15} to 2^{15} - 1 The short type can also be used to save memory. Its default value is 0. **Example: short s = 500;**
int (32 bits)	-2^{31} to 2^{31} - 1 The int type can be used for bigger values. Its default value is 0. **Example: int i = 2500;**
long (64 bits)	-2^{63} to 2^{63} - 1 The long type can be used when you need a range of values wider than those of int. Its default value is 0. **Example: long l = 23333333333;**
Floating-point Type	
float (32)	~ -3.4 x 10^{38} to ~ 3.4 x 10^{38} The float type can be used when floating-point types and values are needed. **Example: float f = 1.4f**
double (64)	~ -1.8 x 10^{308} to ~1.8 x 10^{308} The double type can be used when floating-point types and values are needed. double is a default choice for decimal values. **Example: double d = 22.3;**
Character Type	
char (16)	0 to 65,535 The char type can be used by character types like a, b, c, d, $ Characters of type char are always inside single quotes. For the type char you can use a Unicode character as 'B' or as a hexadecimal number of '\u0000' to '\uFFFF'.

	Examples: '\u03A9' = Ω '\u0045' = E '\u20AC' = € **Example: char letter = 'd';**
Boolean Type	
boolean (1)	The boolean type has two possible values either **true** or **false**. It is false by default. **Example: boolean bool = true;**
String	A string is used for the texts in Java, it is not a primary variable, but it is an object. This book covers string in a separate chapter. Texts of the type string are between double quotes. **Example: String text = "My name is John";**

Data Type	Default Value
byte, short, int, long	0
float, double	0.0
char	'\u0000' (the null character)
boolean	false
non-primitive data types (object)	null Objects are explained later in this book.

2.2 Declaring And Initializing Variables

Variable type (always required)
Identifier (always required)
Initial value (not always required)

Example 1
```
double price = 44.00;
int height;
```

The variable height has the default value of 0, because it is not initialized.
There are three types of variables in Java, namely local variables, instance variables and class variables.

Instance variables: An instance variable is declared within a class, but outside of the methods, constructors or other blocks.
Local variables: A local variable is a variable that is declared within a method, constructor or a block.
Class variables: Class variables are also called static variables. They are declared once inside a class but outside the methods, constructors or blocks. There is only one copy of the class variable is available.

Example 2

```java
class MyClass
{
  double wage;         // instance variable
  static int counter;  // class variable

  void myMethod()      // method
  {
    char gender = 'm'; // local variable
  }
}
```

Quiz 1: Primitive data types and variables

What happens when the following program is compiled and run?

```java
class Worker
{
  boolean isMarried;
  int age = 29;
  long bankAccount = 6552;
  double wage = 110.30;
  char gender = 'm'; // female: f, male: m

  public static void main(String[] args)
  {
    Worker wk = new Worker();

    System.out.print(wk.age + ", ");
    System.out.print(wk.bankAccount + ", ");
    System.out.print(wk.wage + ", ");
    System.out.print(wk.isMarried + ", ");
    System.out.print(wk.gender);
  }
}
```

Select the correct answer:
   a)   This code writes "29, 6552, 110.3, false, m" to the standard output.
   b)   This code writes "29, 6552, 110.3, true, m" to the standard output.

Explanation
All the values of the variables are printed to the standard output.
Since boolean variable "isMarried" is not initialized, its value is by default false.

The correct answer is a.

Exercises

Declare a variable with the name **isForeigner** to know which workers are foreigners.

We assume that the most workers are foreigners.

Add a statement to the program to write the value of the variable **isForeigner** to the standard output.

Change the position of your previous statement in the code to see what happens.

Try to assign the new values 45, 298888888, 124.89, to the variables age, bank account, and wages. What is written to the standard output if the program is compiled and run?

Quiz 2: Primitive data types and variables

What happens when the following program is compiled and run?

```java
class MyVariable
{
    byte b = 80;
    short s;
    float f1 = 3.50f;
    float f2;
    double d;

    public static void main(String[] args)
    {
        MyVariable mv = new MyVariable();

        System.out.print(mv.b + ", ");
        System.out.print(mv.s + ", ");
        System.out.print(mv.f1 + ", ");
        System.out.print(mv.f2 + ", ");
        System.out.print(mv.d);
    }
}
```

Select the correct answer:
  a) This code writes "80, 0, 3.5, 0.0, 0.0" to the standard output.
  b) This code writes "80, 0, 3.5, 0, 0" to the standard output.
  c) This code writes "80, 0, 3.5, 0.0, 0" to the standard output.

Explanation

The default value of integers is "0", but the default value of floats and doubles are "0.0".

The correct answer is a.

Exercises

Assign the new values 122, 43.9f, 335.35 to the variables b, f2, d, and execute the program to see what happens.

Declare a character type variable called "myChar".

Assign the value "Q" to the variable "myChar".

Add a statement to the code to print the value of myChar to the standard output.

Change the position of your statement in the code to see what happens.

Quiz 3: Primitive data types default values

What happens when the following program is compiled and run?

```java
class MyClass
{
    int i;
    double d;
    boolean b;

    public static void main(String[] args)
    {
        MyClass mc = new MyClass();

        System.out.print(mc.i + ", ");
        System.out.print(mc.d + ", ");
        System.out.print(mc.b);
    }
}
```

Select the correct answer:
  a) This code writes "0, 0, false" to the standard output.
  b) This code writes "0, 0.0, false" to the standard output.

Explanation

The correct answer is b, because the default value of double is "0.0".

The correct answer is b.

Exercises

Declare a variable called "myVar", and assign the value 1344.98 to it.

Declare a variable called "myVar2" directly under myVar, and assign the value "g" to it.

Declare a variable called "myVar3" directly under myVar2, and assign the value 766 to it.

Add three statements to the the program to write the values of myVar, myVar2 and myVar3 to the standard output.

Quiz 4: Assigning values to variables

What happens when the following program is compiled and run?

```
class MyClass
{
    int i1 = 7;
    int i2 = 12;

    public static void main(String[] args)
    {
        MyClass mc = new MyClass();

        mc.i1 = mc.i1 - 3;
        mc.i2 = mc.i2 + mc.i1;

        System.out.print(mc.i1 + ", ");
        System.out.print(mc.i2 + " ");
    }
}
```

Select the correct answer:
a) This code writes "7, 12" to the standard output.
b) This code writes "4, 19" to the standard output.
c) This code writes "4, 16" to the standard output.
d) This code writes "7, 19" to the standard output.
e) This program does not compile.

Explanation
i1 = i1 - 3 = 7- 3 = 4. the new value of i1 is 4, and that is why we use this value in the second equation, i2 = i2 + i1 = 12 + 4 = 16.

The correct answer is c.

Exercises
Add the statement "i1 = 9;" directly under the statement "public static void main(String[] args)".
Add the statement "i2 = 8;" directly under the previous statement.
What is written to the standard output if you compile and run the program?

3. Operators

Operators are special symbols that are used to operate on one, two or three operands and return a result. An example is:

age >= 40

In the previous example, age and 40 are operands of >=.
Java supports different types of operators such as: **arithmetic**, **relational**, **conditional**, **assignment**, **unary** and **comparison**.

3.1. Arithmetic Operators

Arithmetic operators are used by working with numbers and mathematical expressions.

Arithmetic operators	Description
+ (Addition)	3 + 6 returns 9
- (subtraction)	8 – 6 returns 2
* (Multiplication)	4 * 5 returns 20
/ (Division)	20/4 returns 5
% (Modulus)	Divides left operand by right operand and returns remainder 17 % 5 returns 2, because 17/5 = 3 and the rest is 17 – (5 * 3) = 2

3.2. Relational Operators

Relational operators are used by evaluating two operands for equality. The answer is either true or false.

Relational Operators	Description
== Equal	Checks the value of two operands. If they are equal returns true else returns false. int x = 5, int y = 6; (x == y) returns false.
!= Not equal	Checks the value of two operands. If they are not equal returns true else returns false. int x = 5, int y = 6; (x != y) returns true.
> Greater than	If the left operand value greater than the right one returns true else returns false. (8 > 5) returns true.

< Less than	If the left operand value is smaller than the right one returns true else returns false. (8 < 5) returns false.
>= Greater or equal	If the left operand value is greater or equal to the right one, returns true else returns false. (7 >= 7) returns true.
<= Less than or equal	If the left operand value is smaller or equal to the right one returns true else returns false. (6 <= 9) returns true

3.3. Conditional Operators

Conditional operators are used by conditional statements. The conditional statement types that Java supports are AND (&&) and OR(| |)

Conditional operators	Description

&& AND	&& combines two boolean variables and returns true only if both of its operands are true.
	 if (3 > 2 && 4 < 6) returns true
	 if(6 > 3 && 3 < 2) returns false

| | OR	| | combines two boolean variables and returns true if one or both of its operands are true. If(1 > 2 | | 6 < 13) returns true

? :	Ternary operator
	 Shorthand formulas
	 if-then-else statement
	 int n = 6;
	 int p = (n == 6) ? 4 :5;
	 The above statement means the following.
	
	 if(n == 6) {
	   p = 4;
	 }
	 else {
	   p = 5;
	 }
	 Returns 4, because n is equal to 6.

3.4 Assignment Operators

Assignment operators	Description
= Assignment operator	Assigns values to variables. x = a - b assigns the value of a - b to x
+= Addition Assignment	x += 5 is equivalent to x = x + 5
-= Subtraction Assignment	x -= 4 is equivalent to x = x – 4
*= Multiplication Assignment	x *= 3 is equivalent to x = x * 3
/= Division Assignment	x /= 2 is equivalent to x = x/2

%= Modulus Assignment	x %= 2 is equivalent to x = x % 2
	example 1
	int x = 21;
	x % 4; is equivalent to x = x % 4
	= 21 % 4 = 1.
	x = 21 % 4 = the rest of 21 divided by 4 = 1.
	
	example 2
	int x = 17;
	x % 3; means x = de rest van 17/3 = 2.

3.5. Unary operators

Unary operators	Description
++ Increment	Increments a value by 1. int x = 20; ++ x returns 21
- - Decrement	Decrements a value by 1 int x = 20; - - x returns 19
!	! reverses the value of a boolean expression. boolean isDefected = false; ! isDefected returns true.

3.6. Type Comparison Operator

Comparison operator	Description
instanceof	Compares an object to a specified type. Objects are later explained in this book.

3.7. The If-Block

The blocks of if-statements are only executed if the condition is true.

The following program writes XU to the standard output.

Example 1

```java
class IfBlock
{
  public static void main(String[] args)
  {
    int x = 6;

    if (x != 6)
    {
      /*
       * this block is being ignored. N is not written to
       * the standard output, since the value of x is equal to 6
       * the program checks further the next block
       */
      System.out.print("N");
    }
    if (x <= 22)
    {
      /*
       * writes Y to the standard output,
       * because the value of x is less than 22
       * the program checks further the next block
       */
      System.out.print("Y");
    }
    if (x < 8 && x != 5)
    {
      /*
       * writes U to the standard output, because
```

```
   * the value of x is smaller than 8 and
   * its value is not equal to 5
   */
   System.out.print("U");
  }
 }
}
```

Example 2

This code is an example of a ternary operator. When the following code is compiled and run "12" is written to the standard output. The shorthand formula of the following code is as follows.

int x = 8;

if(x > 8)
{
    y = 9;
}
else
{
    y = 12;
}

The answer is y = 12, because x is not greater than 8.

```
class TernaryOperator
{
  public static void main(String[] args)
  {
    int x = 8;
    int y = (x > 8) ? 9 : 12;
    System.out.println(y);
  }
}
```

Quiz 1: Arithmetic operators

What happens when the following program is compiled and run?

```
class Calculate
{
  public static void main(String[] args)
  {
    int x = 20;
    int y = 5;
```

```java
    int z = 3;
    double d = 2.2;
    double d2 = 3.7;

    System.out.print(x / y + ", ");
    System.out.print(x * z + ", ");
    System.out.print(x + y - z + ", ");
    System.out.print(x / y + z * 2 + ", ");
    System.out.print(d2 - d);
  }
}
```

Select the correct answer:

    a)   This code writes "4, 60, 22, 10, 1.5" to the standard output.

    b)   This code writes "4, 60, 22, 14, 1.5 " to the standard output.

Explanation

This exercise is a simple calculation.

x/y = 20/5 = 4;

x*z = 20*3 = 60;

x+y-z = 20+5-3 = 22;

x/y + z*2 = 20/5 + 3*2 = 4 + 6 = 10;

d2- d = 3.7-2.2 = 1.5;

The correct answer is a.

Exercises

What does each of the following three statements write to the standard output if you add them directly under the statement System.out.println(d2 - d);

```java
System.out.print(x * y / 10 + ", ");
System.out.print(2 * d2 + 2.5 + ", ");
System.out.print(z * 3 - 6);
```

Quiz 2: Modulus

What happens when the following program is compiled and run?

```java
class MyClass
{
  public static void main(String[] args)
  {
    System.out.print(21 % 7 + ", ");
    System.out.print(12 % 5 + ", ");
```

```
      System.out.print(23 % 6);
   }
}
```

Select the correct answer:

   a) This code writes "3, 2, 3" to the standard output.
   b) This code writes "0, 2, 5" to the standard output.
   c) This code writes "3, 2, 5" to the standard output.

Explanation
Modulus % calculates the remainder of the left-hand operand divided by the right one.

$21/7 = 3$. The remainder is $21 - (3 * 7) = 0$.
$12/5 = 2$. The remainder is $12 - (5 * 2) = 12 - 10 = 2$.
$23 \% 6 = 3$. The remainder is $23 - (6 * 3) = 23 - 18 = 5$

The correct answer is b.

Exercises
What does each of the following three statements write to the standard output if you add them directly under the statement System.out.println(23 % 6);.

System.out.print(44 % 10 + ", ");
System.out.print(7 % 2 + ", ");
System.out.print(30 % 3);

Quiz 3: Increments & decrements

What happens when the following program is compiled and run?

```
class MyClass
{
   public static void main(String[] args)
   {
      int x = 4;
      int y = 6;
      x--;
      y++;
      System.out.print(x + ", " + y);
   }
}
```

Select the correct answer:

   a) This code writes "4, 7" to the standard output.
   b) This code writes "4, 6" to the standard output.
   c) This code writes "3, 7" to the standard output.

d) This code writes "3, 6" to the standard output.

Explanation

x = 4 and y = 6.

x-- decrements the value of x by 1.

x = x - 1 = 4 -1 = 3;

y++ increments the value of y by 1.

y = y + 1 = 6 + 1 = 7

The correct answer is c.

Exercises

Research the following and execute the program to check out your expectation.

Add the statement x++; directly under the statement System.out.print(x + ", " + y);.

Change the position of the statement x++; directly above the statement System.out.print(x + ", " + y);.

Does the position of the statement x++; in de code make any difference?

Quiz 4: Relational operators

What happens when the following program is compiled and run?

```java
class MyClass
{
  public static void main(String[] args)
  {
    int x = 3;
    int y = 8;
    int z = 3;

    if (x == z)
    {
      System.out.print("N");
    }
    if (x >= y)
    {
      System.out.print("O");
    }
    if (x <= z)
    {
      System.out.print("P");
    }
    if (z > y)
    {
      System.out.print("Q");
```

```
    }
    if (y != z)
    {
        System.out.print("R");
    }
  }
}
```

Select the correct answer:
   a) This code writes "NOPQR" to the standard output.
   b) This code writes "NR" to the standard output.
   c) This code writes "NPR" to the standard output.
   d) This code writes nothing to the standard output.

Explanation
The conditional statement if(x == z) returns true, because both variables are equal to 3.
N will be printed to the standard output.
The conditional statement if(x >= y) returns false because x is not greater or equal to y.
The conditional statement if(x <= z) returns true, because x is equal to z and equal to 3.
The letter P is written to the standard output.
The conditional statement if(z > y) is false because z = 3, but y = 8.
The conditional statement if(y != z) is true because z doesn't equal to y.
The letter R is written to the standard output.

The correct answer is c.

Exercises
What is written to the standard output if you make the following changes?
Assign a new value 15 to the variable x and add the statement
System.out.print("Z"); directly under the statement System.out.print("O");
Execute the program to check out your expectation.

Quiz 5: Conditional operators

What happens when the following program is compiled and run?

```
class MyClass
{
  public static void main(String[] args)
  {
    boolean isDefect = true;
    int x = 2;
    int y = 7;
    int z = 9;
```

```java
if (x < y && x > 1)
{
   System.out.print("N");
}
if (z > y || x > y)
{
   System.out.print("O");
}
if (!isDefect)
{
   System.out.print("P");
}
}
}
```

Select the correct answer:
   a) This code writes "NO" to the standard output.
   b) This code writes "OP" to the standard output.
   c) This code writes "NP" to the standard output.

Explanation

The condition if(x < y && x > 1) returns true, because both operands are true.

The condition if(z > y || x > y) returns true, because the operand z > y is true.

|| (conditional or) returns true if one or both operands are true.

The condition if(! isDefect) returns false, because isDetected is true and the sign ! reverses the value of the boolean.

The correct answer is a.

Exercises

What is written to the standard output if you make the following changes to the program?
Compile and run the code to check out your expectation.
Assign the value false to the variable isDefect.
Assign the value 1 to the variable x.

Quiz 6: Conditional operators

What happens when the following program is compiled and run?

```java
class MyClass
{
   public static void main(String[] args)
   {
      boolean isOld = false;
      int x = 5;
      int y = 14;
```

```
    int z = 18;

    if (y > x && z > y && (x + 12) >= z)
    {
       System.out.print("P");
    }
    if (x >= 6 || z <= y || z <= 18)
    {
       System.out.print("Q");
    }
    if (!isOld || y > z)
    {
       System.out.print("R");
    }
  }
}
```

Select the correct answer:
  a) This code writes "PR" to the standard output.
  b) This code writes "QR" to the standard output.
  c) This code writes "PQR" to the standard output.
  d) This code writes "PQ" to the standard output.

Explanation
The condition if(y > x && z > y && (x + 12) >= z) returns false, because one of the operands namely (x + 12) >= z returns false.
The condition if(x >= 6 || z <= y || z <= 18) returns true, because one of the operands return true namely z <= 18.
if(! isOld || y > z) returns true, because one of the operands namely !isOld is true.

The correct answer is b.

Exercises
What is written to the standard output if you make the following changes to the program?
Compile and run the code to check out your expectation.
Assign the value "true" to the variable isOld.
Assign the value "17" to the variable "z".

Quiz 7: Assignment operators

What happens when the following program is compiled and run?

```
class MyClass
{
  public static void main(String[] args)
  {
```

```
    int i1 = 3;
    int i2 = 5;
    int i3 = 12;
    int i4 = 20;
    i1 += 4;
    i2 *= 3;
    i3 /= 3;
    i4 -= 12;

    System.out.print(i1 + ", ");
    System.out.print(i2 + ", ");
    System.out.print(i3 + ", ");
    System.out.print(i4 + " ");
  }
}
```

Select the correct answer:

    a) This code writes "3, 5, 12, 20" to the standard output.
    b) This code writes "4, 3, 3, 12" to the standard output.
    c) This code writes "7, 15, 3, 8" to the standard output.
    d) This code writes "7, 15, 4, 8 " to the standard output.

Explanation

i1 += 4 is equivalent to i1 = i1 + 4 = 3 + 4 = 7
i2 *= 3 is equivalent to i2 = i2 * 3 = 5 * 3 = 15
i3 /= 3 is equivalent to i3 = i3 / 3 = 12 / 3 = 4
i4 -= 12 is equivalent to i4 = i4 - 12 = 20 - 12 = 8

The correct answer is d.

Exercises

What is written to the standard output if you add the following statements to the program?
Compile and run the code to check out your expectation.
Add the following statements directly under the statement i4 -= 12;.
i1 ++ ;
i2 -= 3;
i3 *= 2;
i4 /= 4;

Quiz 8: Assignment operators

What happens when the following program is compiled and run?

```
class MyClass
{
  public static void main(String[] args)
```

```
{
    int i1 = 22;
    int i2 = 17;
    int i3 = 30;
    i1 %= 6;
    i2 %= 5;
    i3 %= 6;

    System.out.print(i1 + " ");
    System.out.print(i2 + " ");
    System.out.print(i3 + " ");
  }
}
```

Select the correct answer:
 a) This code writes "3, 3, 5" to the standard output.
 b) This code writes "4, 2, 0" to the standard output.
 c) This code writes "3, 3, 1" to the standard output.
 d) This code writes "2, 2, 0" to the standard output.

Explanation
22 %= 6. is equal to 4
17%= 5 is equal to 2
30%= 3 is equal to 0

The correct answer is b.

Exercises
What is written to the standard output if you add the following statements to the program? Compile and run the program to check out your expectation.

Add the following statements directly under the statement i3 %= 6;.

i1 %= 3;
i2 %= 7;

Quiz 9: Ternary operator

What happens when the following program is compiled and run?

```
class MyClass
{
  public static void main(String[] args)
  {
    int x = 3;
    int x2 = 8;
```

```
    int y = (x == 3) ? 24 : 8;
    int z = (x2 == 4) ? 33 : 21;
    System.out.print(y);
    System.out.print(z);
  }
}
```

Select the correct answer:
- a) This code writes "833" to the standard output.
- b) This code writes "2433" to the standard output.
- c) This code writes "821" to the standard output.
- d) This code writes "2421" to the standard output.

Explanation

The statement int y = (x == 3) ? 24: 8; is equivalent to:

if x is equal to 3, y is equal to 24;

if x is not equal to 3, y is equal to 8.

This returns 24, because x is equal to 3.

The statement int y = (x2 == 4) ? 33 : 21; returns 21, because x2 is not equal to 4.

The correct answer is d.

Exercises

Assign the value 6 to the variable x and 4 to the variable x2. Wat is written to the standard output if you compile and run the program?

4. Conditional Statements

4.1. if statements

The **if** statement tells the program to execute a certain block of code only if the condition is true.

In the following example the statement if(x != 11) returns false. Therefore the body of the block is ignored. The letter A is not written to the standard output.

The statement if(x > = 8) returns true, therefore the second block is executed, and the letter B is written to the standard output.

The statement if(x <= 13) returns true, therefore the third block is executed. The letter C is written to the standard output.

The statement if(x >= 17) returns false. Therefore the fourth block is ignored. The letter D is not written to the standard output. The output of the following code is: BC

Example 1
```java
class MyClass
{
  public static void main(String[] args)
  {
    int x = 11;
    // block 1
    if (x != 11)
    {
      System.out.print("A");
    }
    // block 2
    if (x >= 8)
    {
      System.out.print("B");
    }
    // block 3
    if (x <= 13)
    {
      System.out.print("C");
    }
    // block 4
    if (x >= 17)
    {
      System.out.print("D");
    }
  }
}
```

4.2. if/else statements

The **if** statement allows executing a certain block of code only if the condition is evaluated as true. If the condition returns false, the **else** block will be executed. In the following example,

The statement if(z != 9) returns true. Therefore the first block is executed. The letter X is written to the standard output.

The statement if(z >= 8) returns true. Therefore the second block is executed. The letter Y is written to the standard output.

The else block (block 3) is not executed because the last if-block (block 2) returns true.

The letter Z is not written to the standard output.

Example 2
```
class MyClass
{
  public static void main(String[] args)
  {
    int z = 8;
    // Block 1
    if (z != 9)
    {
      System.out.print("X");
    }
    // Block 2
    if (z >= 8)
    {
      System.out.print("Y");
    }
    // Block 3
    else
    {
      System.out.print("Z");
    }
  }
}
```

4.3. if-/else-if statements

By working with a ladder of **if/ else-if** statements, the program starts with the first **if** statement. As soon as a block is evaluated as true, the block associated with that statement is executed. The remaining part of the ladder is ignored by the program. If the condition returns false, the block is ignored, and the program continues with the next **else-if** statement. As soon as a block is evaluated as true, the block is executed and the program will ignore the remaining part of the else-if series.

In the following example, The statement if(y == 9) returns false Therefore the first block is ignored, and P is not written to the standard output. The program continues with the next statement.

The statement if(y >= 3) returns true, therefore the second block is executed.

The letter Q is written to the standard output. The rest of the blocks are ignored, regardless whether the conditions return true or false.

Example 3
```java
class MyClass
{
  public static void main(String[] args)
  {
    int y = 6;
    // block 1
    if (y == 9)
    {
      System.out.print("P");
    }
    // block 2
    else if (y >= 3)
    {
      System.out.print("Q");
    }
    // block 3
    else if (y > 4)
    {
      System.out.print("R");
    }
    // block 4
    else
    {
      System.out.print("S");
    }
  }
}
```

4.4. Switch-/Case Statements

The switch statement is used to make a choice from several options. In such cases, if-else statements are not handy, because you need to write a lot of statements to achieve the same goal that can be easier achieved with a switch statement. See example 4. A switch statement starts with the keyword switch.

4.5. Switch-Expression

The switch expression starts after the keyword switch in switch statements. A switch expression is between parentheses. The switch expression must be of type int , char , byte, or short. An example is: switch(day) .

4.6. Case-Label

The constants that are behind the word case are case-labels. The case labels are of the same variable type as the switch-expression, and they are ended with a colon.

Examples
case 1: // A switch expression of the type int
case 'g': // A switch expression of the type char

4.7. Break Statements

Without the break statement, the next case statement is executed. In most cases, each case statement should use a break statement.

4.8. Default Options

The default option is usually the last option in a switch statement. If none of the cases match the switch expression, the default block will be executed. In example 4, an integer variable is declared, for the days of the week.
The day Sunday is 1, Monday is 2, and so on. If the variable day is equal to 1, the statement after case, 1 is executed. In this case, Sunday is written to the standard output. If the variable day is equal to 5, the statement under case 5 is executed. In this case Thursday is written to the standard output, and so on.
If you choose a number that will not match with any of the case labels, the default statement is executed. In that case, Invalid is written to the standard output.
Note that the execution of the program continues with the rest of the cases if you remove all the break statements. In example 4, the day is an integer variable that is equal to 5. Therefore, the statement after case 5 is executed, and Thursday is written to the standard output. The program will not continue with the execution of the rest of the statements because case 5 is ended with a break statement.

Example 4
```java
class Days
{
  public static void main(String[] args)
  {
    int day = 5;

    switch (day)
    {
      case 1:
        System.out.print("Sunday");
        break;
      case 2:
        System.out.print("Monday");
```

```java
        break;
      case 3:
        System.out.print("Tuesday");
        break;
      case 4:
        System.out.print("Wednesday");
        break;
      case 5:
        System.out.print("Thursday");
        break;
      case 6:
        System.out.print("Friday");
        break;
      case 7:
        System.out.print("Saturday");
        break;
      default:
        System.out.print("Invalid");
    }
  }
}
```

You can also write the cases behind each other, as you see in example 5. If the variable day is equal to 1, 2, 3, 4 and 5, the word Business day is written to the standard output. If the variable day is equal to 6 or 7 the word Weekend is written to the standard output. For all other numbers, the word Invalid is written to the standard output.

Example 5

```java
class Days
{
  public static void main(String[] args)
  {
    int day = 4;

    switch (day)
    {
      case 1: case 2: case 3: case 4:
      case 5:
        System.out.print("Business day.");
        break;
      case 6:
      case 7:
        System.out.print("Weekend.");
        break;
```

```
      default:
        System.out.print("Invalid");
    }
  }
}
```

You can write the previous program using if-else-statements.

Example 6
```
class Days
{
  public static void main(String[] args)
  {
    int day = 4;

    if (day > 0 && day <= 5)
    {
      System.out.print("Business day.");
    }
    else if (day == 6 || day == 7)
    {
      System.out.print("Weekend.");
    }
    else
    {
      System.out.print("Invalid.");
    }
  }
}
```

Quiz 1: if statements

What happens when the following program is compiled and run?

```
class MyClass
{
  public static void main(String[] args)
  {
    int i = 2;

    if (i > 0)
    {
      System.out.print("X");
      System.out.print("Y");
```

```
      }
   if (i > 3)
      {
         System.out.print("Z");
      }
   }
}
```

Select the correct answer:
   a) This code writes "X" to the standard output.
   b) This code writes "XY" to the standard output.
   c) This code writes "Z" to the standard output.
   d) This code writes "XYZ" to the standard output.

Explanation
The statement if(i > 0) is true, therefore the block is executed.
The statement System.out.print("X"); writes X to the standard output.
The statement System.out.print("Y"); writes Y to the standard output.
The statement if(i > 3) is false, because i is equal to 2, therefore this if block is ignored.

The correct answer is b.

Exercises
Add your own conditional statement to the program, and check out whether i is equal to 2.
If your statement is true, the program should write "NXY" to the standard output.
Compile and run the program to check out your expectation.

Quiz 2: if statements

What happens when the following program is compiled and run?

```
class MyClass
{
   public static void main(String[] args)
   {
      int a = 3;
      int b = 1;
      int x = 0;

      if (a > b)
      {
         x++;
         if (a > x)
         {
            x += 5;
         }
```

```
        x -= 4;
    }
    if (b == a)
    {
        x += 2;
        if (x < b)
        {
            x += 3;
        }
    }
    System.out.print(x);
    }
}
```

Select the correct answer:
   a) This code writes "0" to the standard output.
   b) This code writes "1" to the standard output.
   c) This code writes "3" to the standard output.
   d) This code writes "2" to the standard output.

Explanation

The statement if(a > b) is true. Therefore, the program executes the block.

The statement x++; adds one to the initial value of x.

x = 0 + 1.

The statement if(a > x) returns true.

The statement x += 5; adds 5 to the value of x.

x = 1 + 5= 6

The statement x -= 4; is equivalent to x = x - 4 = 6 – 4 = 2.

The next if block is:

if(b == a) which returns false. That is why the whole block is ignored.

The correct answer is d.

Exercises

Add your own conditional statement to the program, and check out whether the variable a is equal or smaller than 4.
   1. If your statement returns true, the program should write 2G to the standard output.
   2. Compile and run the program to check out your expectation.

Quiz 3: if-else statements

What happens when the following program is compiled and run?

```
class MyClass
{
    public static void main(String[] args)
```

```java
{
   char c1 = 'g';
   char c2 = 'h';

   if (c1 == 'k')
   {
      System.out.print('w');
   }
   if (c2 == 'h')
   {
      System.out.print('x');
      System.out.print('p');
   }
   if (c1 != c2)
   {
      System.out.print('y');
   }
   else
   {
      System.out.print('z');
   }
}
}
```

Select the correct answer:
  a) This code writes "x" to the standard output.
  b) This code writes "xpy" to the standard output.
  c) This code writes "y" to the standard output.
  d) This code writes "xz" to the standard output.
  e) This code writes "xy" to the standard output.

Explanation

The first statement if(c1 == 'k') is false, therefore the block is ignored.

The Second statement if(c2 == 'h') is true, therefore the block is executed.

The letters x and p is printed to the standard output.

The third statement if(c1 != c2) is true, and the letter y is printed to the standard output.

The last if statement is true, which is why the else block will not be executed.

The correct answer is b.

Exercises
  1. Add your own conditional statement to the program, and check out whether c1 is equal to 'd'.
  2. If your statement is false, the program should write "xpyz" to the standard output.
  3. Note that position of your control statement is important.
  4. Compile and run the program to check out your expectation.

Quiz 4: if/else-if statements

What happens when the following program is compiled and run?

```java
class MyClass
{
  public static void main(String[] args)
  {
    int a = 2;
    int b = 2;
    int x = 5;

    if (a == b)
    {
      x++;
    }
    else if (b == 2)
    {
      x += 2;
    }
    else
    {
      x += 3;
    }
    System.out.print(x);
  }
}
```

Select the correct answer:
   a)   This code writes "5" to the standard output.
   b)   This code writes "6" to the standard output.
   c)   This code writes "8" to the standard output.
   d)   This code writes "7" to the standard output.

Explanation
The first statement if(a == b) is true.
The second statement else-if is also true, but it is ignored by the program.
By if-/else-if statements, only the first true condition is executed.
In this example, the first true statement is the first statement.
The statement x++; increments the value of x by one.
x = 5 + 1 = 6

The correct answer is b.

Exercises

Change the first conditional statement to if(a != b) and add your own conditional statement to the program. Check out whether the variable b is equal or greater than 1. Your statement should be somewhere between the first statement if(a != b) and the last else statement.
The program should write X5 to the standard output.

Quiz 5: if/else-if statements

What happens when the following program is compiled and run?

```
class MyClass
{
  public static void main(String[] args)
  {
    int i = 1;
    int i2 = 4;
    int x = 2;

    if (i == (i2 - 3) && i2 > 5)
    {
      x++;
    }
    else if (i2 == 4)
    {
      x += 2;
    }
    else if (i2 > 3)
    {
      x += 3;
    }
    else
    {
      x += 4;
    }
    System.out.print(x);
  }
}
```

Select the correct answer:
   a) This code writes "2" to the standard output.
   b) This code writes "3" to the standard output.
   c) This code writes "4" to the standard output.
   d) This code writes "7" to the standard output.
   e) This code writes "5" to the standard output.

Explanation
The first if statement if(i == (i2 - 3) && i2 > (i + 3)) is false, because i2 is not greater than

$(i + 3)$.
The second statement else-if(i2 == 4) is true, therefore this block is executed. The rest of the blocks are ignored because the first true else-if statement is found.
The statement x += 2 increments the value of x by 2.
x = 2 + 2 = 4.

The correct answer is c.

Exercises
Add another else-if statement to the program that checks out whether i + i2 = 5.
If your statement returns true, the program should write D2 to the standard output.
Compile and run the program to check out your expectation.

Quiz 6: A combination of conditional statements

What happens when the following program is compiled and run?

```java
class MyClass
{
  public static void main(String[] args)
  {
    int i1 = 3;
    int i2 = 9;
    int i3 = 12;
    int x = 0;

    if (x > -1)
    {
      x++;
      if (i3 == (i1 + i2))
      {
        x += 4;
        if (i1 < 5)
        {
          x += 2;
        }
        else if (i2 == 9)
        {
          x++;
        }
        else
        {
          x -= 2;
        }
        x -= 6;
```

```
      }
      if (i3 < 10)
      {
          x += 7;
      }
      else
      {
          x += 5;
      }
    }
    System.out.print(x);
  }
}
```

Select the correct answer:

      a)   This code writes "5" to the standard output.

      b)   This code writes "13" to the standard output.

      c)   This code writes "7" to the standard output.

      d)   This code writes "12" to the standard output.

      e)   This code writes "6" to the standard output.

Explanation

The first statement if(x > - 1) returns true, therefore the block is executed.

The statement x ++; adds one to the value of x.

x = 0 + 1 = 1;

The statement if(i3 == (i1 + i2)) also returns true.

The statement x += 4; adds 4 to the value of x.

x = 1 + 4 = 5;

The statement if(i1 < 5) returns true. The statement x += 2; adds 2 to the value of x.

x = 5 + 2 = 7;

The rest of the if/else-if blocks are ignored. Read the explanation of if/else-if statements.

The statement x -= 6; decrements the value of x by 6.

x = x - 6 = 7 - 6 = 1;

The statement if(i3 < 10) is false, therefore the block is ignored.

The else statement is executed because the last if statement if(i3 < 10) is false.

The statement x += 5; increments the value of x by 5.

x = x + 5 = 1 + 5 = 6;

The correct answer is e.

Exercises

Add another statement System.out.print(x); to this program.

Choose a position that the code writes "76" to the standard output.

Compile and run the program to check out your expectation.

Quiz 7: Conditional statements inside each other

What happens when the following program is compiled and run?

```java
class MyClass
{
  public static void main(String[] args)
  {
    int i = 2;
    int i2 = 5;
    int i3 = 9;
    int x = 3;
    boolean isSlow = true;

    if (isSlow)
    {
      x++;
      if (i >= 2 && i2 > 7)
      {
        x += 4;
        System.out.print("x" + x + ", ");
        if (i3 == 9)
        {
          x += 5;
          System.out.print("x" + x + ", ");
        }
      }
      else
      {
        x += 6;
        System.out.print("x" + x + ", ");
        if (i3 >= 3)
        {
          x += 7;
        }
        System.out.print("x" + x + ", ");
      }
      x += 3;
    }
    System.out.print("x" + x);
  }
}
```

Select the correct answer:

    a)   This code writes "x8, x13, x10, x17, x20" to the standard output.

b) This code writes "x10, x17, x20" to the standard output.
c) This code writes "x8, x13, x16" to the standard output.
d) This code writes "x10, x10, x20" to the standard output.
e) This code writes "x10, x10, x17" to the standard output.

Explanation

The statement if(isSlow) returns true, the block is executed and the statement x++; increments the value of x by 1.

x = 3 + 1 = 4;

The statement if(i >= 2 && i2 > 7) returns false, because i2 is not greater than 7. The block is ignored. The program starts to execute the else block. The statement x += 6; increments the value of x by 6.

x = 4 + 6 = 10;

The statement System.out.print("x" + x + ", "); writes x10 to the standard output.

The statement if(i3 >= 3) returns true, therefore the statement x += 7; adds 7 to the value of x.

x = 10 + 7 = 17;

The statement System.out.print("x" + x + ", "); writes x17 to the standard output.

The statement x+=3; increments the value of x by 3.

x = 17 + 3 = 20.

The statement System.out.print("x" + x); writes x20 to the standard output.

The correct answer is b.

Exercises

What is written to the standard output if you add the statement
System.out.print("x" + x + ", "); to the program directly under the statement x ++.
Compile and run the program to check out your expectation.

Quiz 8: A simple switch statement

What happens when the following program is compiled and run?

```java
class MyClass
{
  public static void main(String[] args)
  {
    int x = 8;

    switch (x)
    {
      case 6:
        x += 5;
      case 7:
        x += 3;
      case 8:
        x += 2;
      case 9:
```

```
            x++;
            break;
        default:
            x += 4;
    }
    System.out.print(x);
  }
}
```

Select the correct answer:
  a) This code writes "8" to the standard output.
  b) This code writes "15" to the standard output.
  c) This code writes "10" to the standard output.
  d) This code writes "11" to the standard output.
  e) This code writes "14" to the standard output.

Explanation
The cases 6, 7 are ignored, because x is equal to 8
case 8 is executed, and the statement x+=2 adds 2 to the initial value of x.
x = 8 + 2 = 10.
case 8 doesn't end with a break statement, therefore case 9 is also executed.
The statement x++; increments the value of x by one.
x = 10 + 1 = 11; case 9 ends with a break statement, therefore the default block is ignored.
The statement System.out.print(x); prints the value of x to the standard output.

The correct answer is d.

Exercises
What is written to the standard output if you remove the break statement?
What is written to the standard output if you add another break statement under the statement x +=2; of the case 8.

Quiz 9: A switch statement to demonstrate the months of the year

What happens when the following program is compiled and run?

```
class Year
{
  public static void main(String[] args)
  {
    int intMonth = 10;
    String strMonth;

    switch (intMonth)
    {
      case 1:
```

```java
            strMonth = "JAN ";
        case 2:
            strMonth = "FEB ";
        case 3:
            strMonth = "MAR ";
        case 4:
            strMonth = "APR ";
        case 5:
            strMonth = "MAY ";
        case 6:
            strMonth = "JUN ";
        case 7:
            strMonth = "JUL ";
        case 8:
            strMonth = "AUG ";
        case 9:
            strMonth = "SEP ";
        case 10:
            strMonth = "OCT ";
        case 11:
            strMonth = "NOV ";
        case 12:
            strMonth = "DEC ";
            break;
        default:
            strMonth = "INVALID ";
    }
    System.out.println(strMonth);
  }
}
```

Select the correct answer:
  a) This code writes "NOV" to the standard output.
  b) This code writes "AUG SEP OCT NOV DEC" to the standard output.
  c) This code writes "OCT NOV DEC" to the standard output.
  d) This code writes "INVALID" to the standard output.
  e) This code writes "DEC" to the standard output.
  f) This code writes "OCT" to the standard output.

Explanation
case 10 matches the variable of the variable intMonth.
OCT is assigned to strMonth, but case 10 is not ended with a break statement.
That is why the case 11 is also executed and the value NOV is assigned strMonth.
Since there is no break in case 11, case 12 is also executed. The value DEC is assigned to strMonth.

The correct answer is e.

Exercises

This program doesn't function correctly. The goal is that for each value of intMonth the program should write the right month symbol to the standard output as follows.

1. If intMonth is equal to 1, the code must write JAN to the standard output.
2. If intMonth is equal to 2, the code must write FEB to the standard output.
3. If intMonth is equal to 3, the code must write MAR to the standard output.
4. If intMonth is equal to 4, the code must write APR to the standard output.
5. If intMonth is equal to 5, the code must write MAY to the standard output.
6. If intMonth is equal to 6, the code must write JUN to the standard output.
7. If intMonth is equal to 7, the code must write JUL to the standard output.
8. If intMonth is equal to 8, the code must write AUG to the standard output.
9. If intMonth is equal to 9, the code must write SEP to the standard output.
10. If intMonth is equal to 10, the code must write OCT to the standard output.
11. If intMonth is equal to 11, the code must write NOV to the standard output.
12. If intMonth is equal to 12, the code must write DEC to the standard output.
13. By other values, the program should write INVALID to the standard output.

Compile and run the program for each value of intMonth to check out your answer.

Quiz 10: A switch statement represents student's grades

What happens when the following program is compiled and run?

```java
public class Examen
{
  public static void main(String args[])
  {
    char grade = 'C';
    switch (grade)
    {
      case 'A':
        System.out.print("Excellent! ");
        break;
      case 'B':
        System.out.print("Very good ");
        break;
      case 'C':
      case 'D':
        System.out.print("Good ");
      case 'E':
        System.out.print("Try again ");
        break;
```

```
        default:
          System.out.print("Invalid ");
      }
    }
  }
```

Select the correct answer:

      a)   This code writes "Good" to the standard output.

      b)   This code writes "Try again" to the standard output.

      c)   This code writes "Invalid" to the standard output.

      d)   This code writes "Good Try again" to the standard output.

      e)   This code writes nothing to the standard output.

Explanation

There are no statements in case C not even a break. Therefore case D is executed.

case D writes Good to the standard output. There is no break in case D, therefore case E is executed. The statement writes Try again to the standard output.

The correct answer is d.

Exercises

This program doesn't function correctly.

      1.   If the variable grade is equal to C, the program should write Good to the standard output.

      2.   If the variable grade is equal to D, the program should write Fair to the standard output.

      3.   What would happen if grade is equal to N? Compile and run the program to check out your expectation.

5. Iteration (Loop) Statements

Iteration or loop statements are used to handle processes that are one or more times repeated. There are three types of loops in Java namely: **for, while** and **do while**.
A loop consists of two parts:

1. A control part: the repetitions are determined in the control part.
2. A body: the body contains the statements that have to be repeated.

5.1. For Loop

The for-loop is used very frequently in Java. If you know in advance how often a loop must be repeated, the for loop is probably the best choice. In the following example, you see that the initial value of the integer variable i is 0. By each execution of the body the statement i ++ increments the value of the variable i by one. The repetition continues as long as the condition i < 4 is true.

In the beginning, the variable i is equal to 0 . The body is executed, and the letter x is written to the standard output.
In the second repetition, the variable i is equal to 1. The body is for the second time executed, and the letter x is again written to the standard output.
In the third iteration, the variable i is equal to 2. The body is for the third time executed, and the letter x is again written to the standard output.
In the fourth iteration, the variable i is equal to 3. The body is for the fourth time is executed, and the letter x is again written to the standard output.

After the fourth repetition the body is no longer executed, because after the fourth time the variable **i** is equal to 4. This loop writes **xxxx** to the standard output.

Example 1
```
class MyClass
{
  public static void main(String[] args)
  {
    for (int i = 0; i < 4; i++) // the control part
    {
      System.out.print("x"); // the body
    }
  }
}
```

5.2. While Loop

The while loop begins with an evaluation of a condition. If the condition returns true, the body will be executed. The execution of the body of the loop is repeated as long as the condition returns true. If the condition returns false the loop will be terminated. In the following example, the variable number is equal to 1. As long as the variable number is smaller than or equal to 5, the body of the loop is executed. If the body is executed the statement number ++; increments the value of the variable number by one. This loop writes 12345 to the standard output.

Example 2

```java
class MyClass
{
  public static void main(String[] args)
  {
    int number = 1;

    while (number <= 5) // the control part
    {
      System.out.print(number); // the body
      number++;
    }
  }
}
```

5.3. Do-While Loop

The body of the do-while loop is executed at least once because the condition is evaluated after executing the body. The execution of the loop is continued until the condition returns false. When the condition is false, the loop is terminated. In the following example, the loop starts with the statement i ++, which increments the value of i by 1. As long as the variable i is unequal to 3, the body of the loop is executed, and the letter z is written to the standard output. The following example writes zz to the standard output.

Example 3

```java
class MyClass
{
  public static void main(String[] args)
  {
    int i = 1;

    do
    {
      i++;
      System.out.print("z"); // the body
    }
    while (i != 3); // the control part
  }
}
```

5.4. The Break Statement

Sometimes there is no need for a loop to continue, once a certain information is found, or a specific goal is achieved. In this kind of cases, we can terminate the loop with the break statement. In the following example, the execution of the loop terminates as soon as the variable i is equal to 7. Without the break statement, the repetition continues as long as the variable i is smaller than 20. The following loop writes 0123456 to the standard output.

Example 4
```
class MyClass
{
  public static void main(String[] args)
  {
    for (int i = 0; i < 20; i++)
    {
      if (i == 7)
      {
        break;
      }
      System.out.print(i);
    }
  }
}
```

5.5. The Continue Statement

The continue statement skips a certain execution of a loop. The following loop writes 12467 to the standard output because the continue statement is used. If the variable i is equal to 3 or 5 the continue statement skips these two iterations, that is why these two numbers are not written to the standard output.

Example 5
```
class MyClass
{
  public static void main(String[] args)
  {
    for (int i = 1; i <= 7; i++)
    {
      if (i == 3 || i == 5)
      {
        continue;
      }
      System.out.print(i);
    }
  }
}
```

5.6. The Label

Labels are used to manage two or more loops within each other. Java supports labels to refer to a specific line of the code. In the following example is a seat number determined by its row number and column number. We are looking for a seat with a row number 1 and column number 3. As soon as the seat is found, the execution of the loops should be terminated. We first try to achieve this with the break statement.

Example 6
```java
class MyClass
{
  public static void main(String[] args)
  {
    for (int row = 1; row < 3; row++)
    {
      for (int col = 1; col < 4; col++)
      {
        if (row == 1 && col == 3)
        {
          System.out.println("row: "+row +" col: "+col+" is found");
          break;
        }
        System.out.println("row: "+row+" col: "+col + ", ");
      }
    }
  }
}
```

After the seat has been found, the outer loop continues with the second row and writes the seats of the second row to the standard output as shown below.

row: 1 col: 1,
row: 1 col: 2,
row: 1 col: 3 is found
row: 2 col: 1,
row: 2 col: 2,
row:2col:3,

To terminate both loops, we need to label the first loop as outer for example. In example 7 we use the statement break outer to terminate the loops when the seat is found.

Example 7
```java
class MyClass
{
  public static void main(String[] args)
  {
    outer:for (int row = 1; row < 3; row++)
```

```
      {
         for (int col = 1; col < 4; col++)
         {
            if (row == 1 && col == 3)
            {
               System.out.println("row: "+row + " col: "+col+" is found");
               break outer;
            }
            System.out.println("row: "+row+" col: "+col+", ");
         }
      }
   }
}
```

If the code of example 7 is compiled and run, it writes the following to the standard output.

row: 1 col: 1,

row: 1 col: 2,

row: 1 col: 3 is found

Quiz 1: While loop statement

What happens when the following program is compiled and run?

```
class MyLoop
{
   public static void main(String[] args)
   {
      int i = 4;

      while (i > 1)
      {
         i--;
         System.out.print(i);
      }
   }
}
```

Select the correct answer:

a) This code writes "4321" to the standard output.

b) This code writes "321" to the standard output.

c) This code writes "432" to the standard output.

d) This code writes "123" to the standard output.

e) This code writes "234" to the standard output.

f) This code writes "1234" to the standard output.

Explanation

The value of i is equal to 4.

The condition while(i > 1) is true, because i = 4.

i-- decrements the value of I by one.

i = 4 - 1 = 3.

The statement System.out.print(i); prints 3 to the standard output.

The condition while(i > 1) is still true, because i = 3.

i-- decrements the value of I by one.

i = 3 - 1 = 2

The statement System.out.print(i); prints 2 to the standard output.

The condition while(i > 1) is still true, because i = 2.

i-- decrements the value of i by one.

i = 2 - 1 = 1

The statement System.out.print(i); prints 1 to the standard output.

The condition while(i > 1) is false, because i = 1.

The loop is terminated.

The correct answer is b.

Exercises

Assign the value 3 to the variable i. What is written to the standard output if you compile and run the program?

Assign the values 1, 2 and 5 to the variable i. Compile and run the program to see what happens.

Quiz 2: While loop statement

What happens when the following program is compiled and run?

```java
class MyLoop
{
  public static void main(String[] args)
  {
    int i = 8;

    while (i > 1)
    {
      i++;
      System.out.print(i);
      i -= 5;
    }
  }
}
```

Select the correct answer:

a) This code writes "95" to the standard output.

b) This code writes "9876543" to the standard output.
c) This code writes "84" to the standard output.
d) This code writes "9753" to the standard output.
e) This code writes "975" to the standard output.
f) This code writes "864" to the standard output.

Explanation

The initial value of i is 8.

The condition while(i > 1 returns true, i++ increments i by one

i = 8 + 1 = 9.

The statement System.out.print(i); prints 9 to the standard output.

i -= 5 decrements i by 5.

i = 9 - 5 = 4.

The condition while(i > 1) is still true, because i is equal to 4.

i = i + 1 = 5.

The statement System.out.print(i); prints 5 to the standard output.

i -= 5 decrements i by 5.

i = 5 - 5 = 0.

The condition while(i > 1) returns false, because i is not greater than 1.

The loop is terminated.

The correct answer is a.

Exercises

If you remove the statement i -= 5 from the program, the program loops endlessly. What is your explanation for that?

Quiz 3: do-While loop

What happens when the following program is compiled and run?

```java
class MyLoop
{
  public static void main(String[] args)
  {
    int i = 2;

    do
    {
      i += 5;
      System.out.print(i);
    }
    while (i <= 12);
  }
}
```

Select the correct answer:
   a)   This code writes "712" to the standard output.
   b)   This code writes "7" to the standard output.
   c)   This code writes "2712" to the standard output.
   d)   This code writes "2" to the standard output.
   e)   This code writes "71217" to the standard output.
   f)   This code writes nothing to the standard output.

Explanation

The first execution of the loop:
The initial value of i is 2.
I += 5; increments I by 5.
i = 2 + 5 = 7.
The statement System.out.print(i); prints 7 to the standard output.
The condition while(i <= 12); is true, because i = 7 and it is smaller than 12

The second execution of the loop:
i = 7 + 5 = 12.
The statement System.out.print(i); prints 12 to the standard output.
The condition while(i <= 12); is still true, because i = 12.

The third execution of the loop:
i = 12 + 5 = 17.
The statement System.out.print(i); prints 17 to the standard output.
The condition while(i <= 12); is false, because i = 17 and it is greater than 12.
The loop is terminated.

The correct answer is e.

Exercises

What is the result if you change the initial value of i to 4 and replace the statement i += 5; with i += 6;?
Compile and run the program to check out your expectation.

Quiz 4: do-While loop

What happens when the following program is compiled and run?

```java
class MyLoop
{
  public static void main(String[] args)
  {
    int i = 1;

    do
    {
      i += 3;
```

```java
        if (i != 4)
        {
           System.out.print("x");
        }
        else
        {
           System.out.print("y");
        }
     }
     while (i != 10);
   }
}
```

Select the correct answer:

    a)   This code writes "xyy" to the standard output.

    b)   This code writes "yxyy" to the standard output.

    c)   This code writes "xxy" to the standard output.

    d)   This code writes "yxxx" to the standard output.

    e)   This code writes "yxx" to the standard output.

    f)   This code writes nothing to the standard output.

Explanation

The first execution of the loop:

The initial value of i is 1, i += 3.

i = 1 + 3 = 4.

The condition if(i != 4) returns false, because i is equal to 4.

The statement System.out.print("y"); prints y to the standard output.

The condition while(i != 10); is true, because i = 4.

The second execution of the loop:

i = 4 + 3 = 7.

The condition if(i != 4) returns true, because i is equal to 7.

The statement System.out.print("x"); prints x to the standard output.

The condition while(i != 10); is true, because i = 7.

The third execution of the loop:

i = 7 + 3 = 10.

The condition if(i != 4) returns true, because i is equal to 10.

The statement System.out.print("x"); prints x to the standard output.

The condition while(i != 10); is false, because i = 10.

The loop is terminated.

The correct answer is e.

Exercises

What happens if you change the initial value of i to 2?

What is written to the standard output if you change the initial value of i to 2, and you replace the statement while(i != 10) with the statement while(i < 10).

Compile and run the program to check out your expectation.

Quiz 5: for loop statement

What happens when the following program is compiled and run?

```
class MyLoop
{
    public static void main(String[] args)
    {
        for (int i = 4; i < 7; i++)
        {
            System.out.print(i);
        }
    }
}
```

Select the correct answer:
   a) This code writes "4567" to the standard output.
   b) This code writes "456" to the standard output.
   c) This code writes "56" to the standard output.
   d) This code writes "567" to the standard output.
   e) This code writes "45" to the standard output.
   f) This code writes "654" to the standard output.

Explanation

The first loop execution:

The condition for(int i = 4; i < 7; i ++) is true, because the initial value of i = 4 and that is smaller than 7. As long as i is smaller than 7 the program adds one to the value of i executes the body of the loop. The statement System.out.print(i); prints 4 to the standard output.

The second loop execution:

The condition for(int i = 4; i < 7; i ++) is still true, because i = 4 + 1 = 5.

5 is smaller than 7.

The statement System.out.print(i); prints 5 to the standard output.

The third loop execution:

The condition for(int i = 4; i < 7; i ++) is still true, because i = 5 + 1 = 6.

6 is smaller than 7.

The statement System.out.print(i); prints 6 to the standard output.

After that the loop is terminated, because i = 6 + 1 = 7 and that is not smaller than 7.

The correct answer is b.

Exercises
What happens when you replace the statement for(int i = 4; i < 7; i ++) with
for(int i = 1; i < 10; i += 3)? Compile and run the program to check out your expectation.

Quiz 6: for loop statement

What happens when the following program is compiled and run?

```java
class MyLoop
{
  public static void main(String[] args)
  {
    int x = 1;

    for (int i = 1; i < 7; i += 2)
    {
      x += i;
    }
    x -= 2;
    System.out.print(x);
  }
}
```

Select the correct answer:
  a) This code writes "8" to the standard output.
  b) This code writes "7" to the standard output.
  c) This code writes "2" to the standard output.
  d) This code writes "5" to the standard output.
  e) This code writes "9" to the standard output.
  f) This code writes "0" to the standard output.

Explanation
The first loop execution:
The condition for(int i = 1; i < 7; i += 2) is true, because the initial value of i = 1 and that is smaller than 7.
As long as i is smaller than 7 execute the body of the loop.
The initial value of x is 1.
x += i, x = 1 + i = 1 + 1 = 2.

The second loop execution:
The condition for(int i = 1; i < 7; i += 2) is ture, because the value of i = 1 + 2 = 3 and that is smaller than 7.

As long as i is smaller than 7 execute the body of the loop.

x += i, x = 2 + i = 2 + 3 = 5.

The third loop execution:

The condition for(int i = 1; i < 7; i += 2) is true, because the value of i = 3 + 2 = 5 and that is smaller than 7.

As long as i is smaller than 7 execute the body of the loop.

x += i, x = 5 + 5 = 5 + 5 = 10.

The condition for(int i = 1; i < 7; i += 2) is now false because i = 5 + 2 = 7 and 7 is not smaller than 7. The loop is terminated.

x -= 2 decreases two from the value of x. x = 10 - 2 = 8.

The statement System.out.print(x); prints the value of x, which is 8 to the standard output.

The correct answer is a.

Exercises

What happens when you replace the statement for(int i = 1; i < 7; i += 2) with the statement for(int i = 3; i < 13; i += 5)? Compile and run the program to check out your expectation.

Quiz 7: for loop and if-else statements

What happens when the following program is compiled and run?

```java
class MyLoop
{
  public static void main(String[] args)
  {
    char c = 'a';
    char c2 = 'b';

    for (int i = 4; i >= 0; i--)
    {
      if (i >= 3 || i == 1)
      {
        System.out.print(c2);
      }
      else
      {
        System.out.print(c);
      }
    }
  }
}
```

Select the correct answer:

   a)   This code writes "baaba" to the standard output.
   b)   This code writes "baab" to the standard output.
   c)   This code writes "aaba" to the standard output.
   d)   This code writes "bbaba" to the standard output.
   e)   This code writes "aabab" to the standard output.
   f)   This code writes "aaba" to the standard output.

Explanation

The first loop execution.

By each execution of the loop body, the value of i decreases by one.

The condition for(int i = 4; i >= 0; i --) is true, the initial value of i = 4.

As long as i is greater or equal to 0 execute the body of the loop.

The initial value of i = 4.

The condition if(i >= 3 || i == 1) returns true. because i is greater than 3.

The statement System.out.print(c2); prints "b" to the standard output.

The second loop execution.

The condition for(int i = 4; i >= 0; i --) is true, i = 4 - 1 = 3.

As long as i is greater or equal to 0 execute the body of the loop.

The value of i = 3.

The condition if(i >= 3 || i == 1) returns true. because i is equal to 3.

The statement System.out.print(c2); prints "b" to the standard output.

The third loop execution.

The condition for(int i = 4; i >= 0; i --) is true, i = 3 - 1 = 2.

As long as i is greater or equal to 0 execute the body of the loop.

The value of i = 2.

The condition if(i >= 3 || i == 1) returns false. because i is equal to 2.

The statement System.out.print(c); prints "a" to the standard output.

The fourth loop execution.

The condition for(int i = 4; i >= 0; i --) is true, i = 2 - 1 = 1.

As long as i is greater or equal to 0 execute the body of the loop.

The value of i = 1.

The condition if(i >= 3 || i == 1) returns true. because i is equal to 1.

The statement System.out.print(c2); prints "b" to the standard output.

The fifth loop execution.

The condition for(int i = 4; i >= 0; i --) is true, i = 1 - 1 = 0.

As long as i is greater or equal to 0 execute the body of the loop.

The value of i = 0.

The condition if(i >= 3 || i == 1) returns false. because i is equal to 0.

The statement System.out.print(c); prints "a" to the standard output. The loop is terminated.

The correct answer is d.

Exercises

What happens when you replace the statement if(i >= 3 || i == 1) with the statement if(i < 2 || i == 4)? Compile and run the program to check out your expectation.

Quiz 8: for loop and break

What happens when the following program is compiled and run?

```java
class MyLoop
{
  public static void main(String[] args)
  {
    int x = 17;
    int y = 3;

    for (int i = 0; i < 10; i++)
    {
      x += 2;
      y += 5;
      if (x >= 21)
      {
        break;
      }
    }
    System.out.print(y);
  }
}
```

Select the correct answer:
  a) This code writes "53" to the standard output.
  b) This code writes "18" to the standard output.
  c) This code writes "13" to the standard output.
  d) This code writes "23" to the standard output.

Explanation
The first loop execution.
The condition for(int i = 0; i < 10; i ++) is true, because the initial value of i = 0 and that is smaller than 10.
As long as i is smaller than 10 the program executes the body of the loop.
The initial value of x is 17.
x += 2, x = 17 + 2 = 19.
The initial value of y = 3;
y = 3 + 5 = 8;
The condition if(x >= 21) is false, because x is smaller than 21.

The second loop execution.

The condition for(int i = 0; i < 10; i ++) is true, because the value of i = 1 and that is smaller than 10.

As long as i is smaller than 10 the program executes the body of the loop.

The value of x is 19.

x += 2, x = 19 + 2 = 21.

The value of y = 8;

y = 8 + 5 = 13;

The condition if(x >= 21) is true, because x is equal to 21.

The break statement is reached and it terminates the loop

The statement System.out.print(y); prints the last value of y to the standard output, which is 13.

The correct answer is c.

Exercises

What happens when you change the initial value of x to 14 and y to 5?

Remove the break statement from the program to see the difference.

Compile and run the program to check out your expectation.

Quiz 9: for loop and continue

What happens when the following program is compiled and run?

```java
class LeapYear
{
  public static void main(String[] args)
  {
    for (int year = 1993; year <= 2001; year++)
    {
      if ((year % 4 != 0))
      {
        continue;
      }
      System.out.print(year + " ");
    }
  }
}
```

Select the correct answer:
   a) This code writes "1993 1994 1995 1996 1997 1998 1999 2000 2001" to the standard output.
   b) This code writes "1994 1996 1998 2000" to the standard output.
   c) This code writes "1996 2000" to the standard output.
   d) This code writes "1993 1994 1995 1997 1998 1999 2001" to the standard output.

e)   This code writes nothing to the standard output.

Explanation

The first loop execution.

The condition for(int year = 1993; year <= 2001; year ++) is true the body of the loop is executed.

The condition if((year % 4 != 0)) means year/4 is not equal to 0.

When the above condition is true, the continue statement ignores that specific year.

When year/4 is equal to 0, the year is written to the standard output.

Only 1996 and 2000 are written to the standard output.

The correct answer is c.

Exercises

Change this program to write all the common (not leap) years between 2016 to 2040 to the standard output.

Remove the continue statement to see the difference.

Compile and run the code to test your changes.

Quiz 10: A combination of two loops

What happens when the following program is compiled and run?

```
class MiniTheater
{
  public static void main(String[] args)
  {
    for (int row = 1; row < 3; row++)
    {
      for (int column = 1; column < 4; column++)
      {
        System.out.print(row + "," + column + " ");
      }
    }
  }
}
```

Select the correct answer:
   a)   This code writes "1,1 2,2 3,3" to the standard output.
   b)   This code writes "1,2 1,3 2,2 2,3" to the standard output.
   c)   This code writes "1,1 1,2 2,1 2,2" to the standard output.
   d)   This code writes "1,1 1,2 1,3 2,1 2,2 2,3" to the standard output.
   e)   This code writes nothing to the standard output.

Explanation

The first-time execution of the outer loop.

The condition for(int row = 1; row < 3; row ++) is true

The initial value of row = 1.

For each value of row, the loop body of the inner (col) loop is executed three times.

when row = 1, col = 1, 2, 3.

The statement System.out.print(row + "," + col + " "); prints 1,1 1,2 1,3 to the standard output.

The second time execution of the outer loop.

The condition for(int row = 1; row < 3; row ++) is true and the value of row is equal to 2.

For each value of row, the inner loop is executed three times.

when row = 2, col = 1, 2, 3.

The statement System.out.print(row + "," + col + " "); prints 2,1 2,2 2,3 to the standard output.

the value of the row is 3, and that is why for(int row = 1; row < 3; row ++) returns false, and the outer loop is terminated followed by the termination of the inner loop.

The correct answer is: 1,1 1,2 1,3 2,1 2,2 2,3

The correct answer is d.

Exercises

In this program, you have two rows and three columns. Change the row numbers to five instead of two. Add a statement to this code to write only the rows 2, 4, 5 to the standard output. The output must be 2,1 2,2 2,3 4,1 4,2 4,3 5,1 5,2 5,3. Compile and run the code to test your changes.

Quiz 11: A combination of two loops with labels

What happens when the following program is compiled and run?

```java
class Theater
{
  public static void main(String[] args)
  {
    outer:for (int row = 1; row < 4; row++)
    {
      for (int column = 1; column < 5; column++)
      {
        if (row == 2 && column == 3)
        {
          break outer;
        }
        System.out.print(row + "," + column + " ");
      }
    }
  }
}
```

Select the correct answer:

    a)   This code writes "1,1 1,2 1,3 2,1 2,2 2,3" to the standard output.

    b)   This code writes "1,1 1,2 1,3 1,4 2,1 2,2" to the standard output.

    c)   This code writes "1,1 1,2 1,3 1,4 2,1 2,2 2,3" to the standard output.

    d)   This code writes "1,1 1,2 1,3" to the standard output.

    e)   This code writes nothing to the standard output.

Explanation

The first-time execution of the outer loop.

The condition for(int row = 1; row < 4; row ++) is true

The initial value of row = 1.

For each value of row, the inner loop is executed four times.

for(int col = 1; col < 5; col ++)

when row = 1, col assigns the values 1, 2, 3, 4.

The statement System.out.print(row + "," + col + " "); prints 1,1 1,2 1,3 1,4 to the standard output.

The second execution of the outer loop.

The condition for(int row = 1; row < 3; row ++) is true and the value of row is equal to 2.

For each value of row, the inner loop is executed four times.

for(int col = 1; col < 5; col ++)

when row = 2, col = 1, 2, 3, 4.

if(row == 2 && col == 3)

break outer; the program jumps to the outer loop and is terminated.

The statement System.out.print(row + "," + col + " "); prints 2,1 2,2 to the standard output.

The correct answer is b.

Exercises

Give the loop for(int col = 1; col < 5; col ++) the label inner, and change the statement break outer; to break inner;. What is written to the standard output if you compile and run the code? Check out your expectation.

6. Classes, Objects & Constructors

6.1. What Is A Class?

A class is a sort template which can be used to instantiate objects. Java programs contain either classes or interfaces, which would be discussed later in this book. Each class has variables and methods, which are called class members. The class name in Java starts with a capital letter. Programmers can choose an appropriate class name. Class name examples are: Worker, Account, and Student.

6.2. What Is An Object?

By creating a class you have only the description, but no objects are created. You can use a class to instantiate as many objects as you want. It is also said that an object is an instance of a class. A class contains variables and methods, while An object is the implementation of a class and represents the data.

The following class Student contains the variables name and gender. The objects of the class Student represent the data, such as: William, man or Sophia woman. The class determines which data you can have about the students.

Example 1
```java
class Student
{
  // instance variable
  String name;
  // instance variable
  char gender = 'm'; // m: male, f: female
}
```

In example 1 we can't access information about William's or Sophia's age because the class Student doesn't contain the attribute age. If you want to know the age of the students, you need to add an extra field to the class Student named age as shown in example 2.

Example 2
```java
class Student
{
  String name;
  char gender = 'm'; // m: male, f: female
  int age;
}
```

6.3. Creating Objects From A Class?

To create an object from a class we use the keyword new as follows:
ClassName objectName = new ClassName();
Student student; // student, is a reference to an object. Keep in mind that the student object is created if you use the statement new Student();. The statement Student student; creates only a reference student. The following statement instantiates the object student from the class Student.
Student student = new Student();

To assign a value to an instance variable, we use the name of the object separated from the variable name by a dot. The following statement assigns the value 25 to the variable age of the object student.

student.age = 25;

To access the variables of the object student we use the name of the object and the name of the variable separated by a dot.
student.age

Example 3

```java
class Student
{
   String name;
   char gender = 'm'; // m: male, f: female
   int age;

   public static void main(String[] args)
   {
     Student st = new Student();

     st.name = "David";
     st.age = 31;
     System.out.println("Name:      " + st.name);
     System.out.println("Gender:    " + st.gender);
     System.out.println("Age:       " + st.age);
   }
}
```

If the previous example is compiled and run, the following is written to the standard output.

Name: David
Gender: m
Age: 31

6.4. Object References

It is allowed in Java to create one or more references to a single object. Below, we create three references namely student, student2, and student3 to an object.

Student student = new Student();
student.name = "Emma";
Student student2 = student;
Student student3 = student2;

All three references student, student2, and student3 refer to the same object, and the value of the variable name of all the three objects is Emma.

student.name is Emma;
student2.name is Emma;
student3.name is Emma;

6.5. What Is A Constructor?

A constructor is a special method that has the same name as the class name in which it exists. You can use a constructor to create an object. You can also use a constructor to initialize the instance variables of a class. This will be explained later in this chapter.

Example 4

```java
class Student
{
    String name;
    char gender = 'm'; // m: male, f: female
    int age;

    // no-argument constructor
    public Student()
    {
    }
}
```

In the previous example, there is a no-argument constructor in the class Student. You can use it to create the object student as follows:

Student student = new Student();

The parentheses can also include variables (arguments). We call the previous Student () constructor a no-argument constructor because the constructor does not contain variables (arguments). In every class, you can call the no-argument constructor when the class doesn't have any constructor. The reason is that the no-argument constructor is automatically arranged by Java.

6.6. How To Define A Constructor ?

It is important to understand that the default (no-argument) constructor, can only call if the class doesn't have any constructor. When you define a constructor with one or more arguments, you can no longer call the default constructor. You can use a constructor with arguments to assign values to the instance variables. In the following class Student a constructor with two arguments is defined, therefore you can no longer call the default constructor to instantiate objects.

If you want to instantiate an object of the class Student, you can call the constructor with two arguments as follows.

Student student = new Student("David", 31);

The statement **this.name = name;** assigns the value of the argument name in this case David to the instance variable name and the statement **this.age = age;** assigns the value 31 to the instance variable age.

Example 5

```java
class Student
{
  String name;
  int age;

  // a constructor with two arguments
  public Student(String name, int age)
  {
    this.name = name;
    this.age = age;
  }
  public static void main(String[] args)
  {
    Student st = new Student("David", 31);
    System.out.println("Name:    " + st.name);
    System.out.println("Age:    " + st.age);
  }
}
```

If the previous code is compiled and run the following is written to the standard output.

Name: David
Age: 31

In the previous example you cannot call the no-argument constructor. If you want to instantiate objects from the class Student by calling the no-argument constructor, you need to add the following constructor to the code.

```java
// no-argument constructor
public Student()
{
}
```

Calling a constructor within another constructor
You can define one or more constructors in one class. It is also possible to call a constructor from another constructor. To call a constructor, within another constructor we use the keyword **this**. In the following example, we call the constructor with two arguments from the constructor with one argument by using the statement this(name, 20);. If you call the one-argument constructor to create an object, the value of 20 is assigned to the variable age. See the following program:

Example 6

```java
class Student
{
  String name;
  int age;

  // one-argument constructor
  public Student(String name)
  {
    // calling the two-argument constructor
    this(name, 20);
  }
  // two-argument constructor
  public Student(String name, int age)
  {
    this.name = name;
    this.age = age;
  }
  public static void main(String[] args)
  {
    Student st = new Student("Emma");
    System.out.println("Name:      " + st.name);
    System.out.println("Age:       " + st.age);
  }
}
```

If you compile an run the program, the following is written to the standard output.

Name: Emma

Age: 20

Quiz 1: Instantiating objects

What happens when the following program is compiled and run?

```java
class Employee
{
  String name = "Anna";
  int age = 22;

  public static void main(String[] args)
  {
    Employee emp = new Employee();
    Employee emp2 = new Employee();

    emp.name = "John";
```

```
      emp.age = 20;
      System.out.print(emp.name + " ");
      System.out.print(emp2.age + " ");
   }
}
```

Select the correct answer:
  a)   This code writes "Anna 22" to the standard output.
  b)   This code writes "John 22" to the standard output.
  c)   This code writes "John 20" to the standard output.
  d)   This code writes "Anna 20" to the standard output.
  e)   This code writes nothing to the standard output.

Explanation
The statement Employee emp = new Employee(); create the object emp.
The statement emp.name = "John"; assigns the value John to the name variable.

The statement Employee emp2 = new Employee(); create the object emp2.
By default, the name and age of all the objects are assigned to Anna and 22.
That is why emp2.age prints 22 to the standard output.

The correct answer is b.

Exercises
  1.   We need to know extra information about each employee namely, their phone numbers and the city where they live.
  2.   Create a new employee object called employee; name is Emma, age 25, phone number 00233-786854 and she lives in New York.
  3.   Add a piece of code to write all the information (including phone number and city) of "Emma" to the standard output.
  4.   Add a piece of code to write all the information about "John" to the standard output. John lives in California and assume that his phone number is 00383-384833

Quiz 2: Objects and object references

What happens when the following program is compiled and run?

```
class MyClass
{
   int x;
   int y = 7;

   public static void main(String[] args)
   {
      MyClass mc = new MyClass();
```

```
    mc.x = 5;
    mc.y = 8;

    MyClass mc2 = new MyClass();
    MyClass mc3 = mc;
    System.out.print(mc.x + ", " + mc2.x + ", " + mc3.y);
  }
}
```

Select the correct answer:
   a) This code writes "5, 0, 8" to the standard output.
   b) This code writes "5, 5, 7" to the standard output.
   c) This code writes "5, 0, 7" to the standard output.
   d) This code writes "5 5 8" to the standard output.
   e) This code writes nothing to the standard output.

Explanation

MyClass contains two variables namely x & y.

The statement MyClass mc = new MyClass(); instantiates the object mc.

mc.x = 5; assigns the value of 5 to x.

The statement MyClass mc2 = new MyClass(); instantiates the object mc2.

The default value of x is 0, because x is not initialized.

mc2.x = 0;

The statement MyClass mc3 = mc; creates a reference mc3 to the object mc.

mc3.y is the same as mc.y, because mc3, mc are both references to the same object.

mc.y = 8, and that is why mc3.y is also equal to 8.

The correct answer is a.

Exercises

   1. Create an object called myClass and refer it to the object mc3.
   2. Add a statement to the program to write the variables x and y of the object myClass to the standard output.

Quiz 3: Three constructors in one class

What happens when the following program is compiled and run?

```
class MyClass
{
  int x = 2;
  int y = 5;

  // no-argument constructor
```

```java
MyClass()
{
}
// one-argument constructor
MyClass(int x)
{
   this.y = x;
}
// two-arguments constructor
MyClass(int x, int y)
{
   this.x = x;
   this.y = y;
}
public static void main(String[] args)
{
   MyClass mc = new MyClass();
   MyClass mc2 = new MyClass(7);
   MyClass mc3 = new MyClass(9, 3);
   System.out.print(mc.y + ", " + mc2.y + ", " + mc3.x);
}
}
```

Select the correct answer:
a) This code writes "5, 7, 2" to the standard output.
b) This code writes "5, 2, 9" to the standard output.
c) This code writes "5, 2, 2" to the standard output.
d) This code writes "5, 7, 9" to the standard output.
e) This code does not compile.

Explanation
The statement MyClass mc = new MyClass(); creates the object mc.
mc.y = 5 the value of y is equal to 5.

The statement MyClass mc2 = new MyClass(7); creates the object mc2 using the one-argument constructor.
The statement this.y = x; assigns 7 to the value of y.

The statement MyClass mc3 = new MyClass(9,3); uses the two-argument constructor.
the value of x assigned to the first arg, which is 9.
this.x = x;

The correct answer is d.

Exercises
1. Call the third (two-argument) constructor within the first constructor so that all the new created objects by default have x = 6 and y = 3.

2. Instantiate a new object called myObject using the first (no-argument) constructor.
3. Add a statement to write both variables x and y of your object myObject to the standard output.

The x value of your object should be 6 and the y value 3.

Quiz 4: Calling a constructor within a constructor

What happens when the following program is compiled and run?

```java
class Staff
{
   String name = "Ron";
   double salary = 400.0;

   Staff(String name)
   {
      this(name, 780.0);
   }
   Staff(String name, double salary)
   {
      this.name = name;
      this.salary = salary;
   }
   public static void main(String[] args)
   {
      Staff st = new Staff("Ben");
      System.out.print(st.name + ", " + st.salary);
   }
}
```

Select the correct answer:
   a) This code writes "Ben, 780.0" to the standard output.
   b) This code writes "Ron, 400.0" to the standard output.
   c) This code writes "Ben, 400.0" to the standard output.
   d) This code writes "Ron, 780.0 Ron 400.0" to the standard output.
   e) This code does not compile.

Explanation
The statement Staff st = new Staff("Ben"); instantiate the object st.
By calling the one-argument constructor the statement this(name,780.0); calls the two-argument constructor.
which assigns new values to the variables name and salary.
name = "Ben";
salary = 780.0;

The correct answer is a.

Exercises

Create n staff object called "staffObject" for Mary, her salary is 2000.55. Use the (two-argument) constructor.

1. Add a statement to the program to write the name and the salary of the staffObject to the standard output.
2. Compile and run the program to check out your answer.

Quiz 5: Calling a constructor within another constructor

What happens when the following program is compiled and run?

```java
class MyClass
{
    int x = 3;
    int y = 5;

    MyClass()
    {
        this(4, 6);
    }
    MyClass(int x, int y)
    {
        this.y = y;
    }
    public static void main(String[] args)
    {
        MyClass mc = new MyClass();
        MyClass mc2 = new MyClass(9, 7);
        System.out.print(mc.x + ", " + mc.y + ", "+ mc2.x + ", " + mc2.y);
    }
}
```

Select the correct answer:
a) This code writes "4, 6, 9, 7" to the standard output.
b) This code writes "3, 5, 9, 7" to the standard output.
c) This code writes "4, 6, 3, 7" to the standard output.
d) This code writes "3, 6, 3, 7" to the standard output.
e) This code does not compile.

Explanation

The statement MyClass mc = new MyClass(); instantiates the mc object.

The no-argument constructor calls the two-argument constructor by using the statement this(4,6);

The two-argument constructor assigns the y parameter to the value of y by using the statement this.y = y;

The value of x is not assigned to the x parameter, and that is why the x value remains the initial value 3.

mc.x = 3;

The statement this(4,6); assigns the value of y to 6. mc.y = 6

The statement MyClass mc2 = new MyClass(9,7); assigns the value of y to 7, but x remains 3.

mc2.x = 3;

mc2.y = 7;

The result is 3, 6, 3, 7

The correct answer is d.

Exercises

1. Add an uninitialized integer variable "z" to the class MyClass.
2. Add a three-argument constructor to MyClass, and pass all the variable x, y, z to it.
3. Use your own created constructor to instantiate an object of MyClass called mc3, and pass the values 7, 8, 9 to it.
4. Add a statement to write the values of the variables to the standard output.

5. Compile and run the program to check out your expectation.

Assignment: Create a class Employee twice

- The first class Employee should define a constructor.
- Second Employee class should not define a constructor.

1. Create a class Employee.
2. We want the following information about the employees: name, salary, and the country of origin. Most employees have a standard monthly salary of $ 2400.55 and most of them are from France.
3. Create the employee object for Olivia who is from Canada and her salary is $ 3100.45.
4. Repeat step 3 for Daniel, his salary is $ 2400.55 and he is from France.
5. Add a piece of code to the program to write all the data of Olivia and Daniel to the standard output. There are two methods to achieve the goal. Write the program first by using a constructor and also without a constructor. The result would be something like the following.

-------- Employees -----------

Name: Olivia

Salary: $ 3100.45

Country: Canada

Name: James

Salary: $ 2400.55

Country: France

7. Methods

Every class in Java has members, namely, variables and methods. You can't write a useful class in Java without methods. In the previous chapters, we avoided writing methods in the classes except for the main method. The reason was because you were not familiar with methods yet. You will learn in this chapter to write different types of methods. Each method has a block code that starts with an opening curly brace and ends with a closing brace. The body of the method contains the code between the curly braces.

A method name in Java begins with a lowercase letter and ends with an open and a close parenthesis. Examples are: getNetSalary( ), setPrice(), getPrice(). The empty parentheses indicate that there are no values passed to the method.

Methods allow you to decide what you want to do with objects. You can call a method using the name of an object followed by the name of the method, separated by a dot. In the following class Item, we define the method getDiscountPrice(). We can call that method by creating an object of the class Item as follows:

Item item = new Item();
item.getDiscountPrice();

There are two types of methods, namely: methods that return a value and methods that doesn't return any value.

7.1. Methods that return a value

If a method reads data, it usually returns a primitive variable or an object. If a variable type or an object type appears before the name of the method, that method returns that variable type. The data type for the name of the method is the same type variable that the method returns. In Java, the keyword return is used before the returned result. As soon as a return statement is reached, the rest of the body of the method is ignored.

In example 1 the method getDiscountPrice calculates the price with a 20% discount. The double variable before the name of the method means that the method returns a value of the type of double.

Example 1
```
class Item
{
  double price = 160.0;

  double getDiscounPrice()
  {
    double discount = price * 0.20;
    double discountPrice = price - discount;
    return discountPrice;
  }
  public static void main(String[] args)
  {
    Item itm = new Item();
    System.out.println("Price with 20% $ " + itm.getDiscounPrice());
```

```
        }
}
```

If the program is compiled and run, it writes the following to the standard output.

Price with 20% $ 128.0

7.2. Methods that doesn't return any value

The methods that you use to set or change values they usually don't return values. If the keyword void appears before the name of the method means that the method doesn't return any value.

With methods that don't return value, you can change or set values of the variables. In the following example, the method setPrice increases the value of the variable price by $ 10. This method doesn't return any value, therefore it begins with the keyword void.

Example 2
```java
class Item
{
  double price = 70.0;

  // the following method changes the price
  void setPrice()
  {
    this.price = 80.0;
  }
  public static void main(String[] args)
  {
    Item itm = new Item();
    System.out.println("The price was: $ " + itm.price);
    // when you invoke the method, the price will be changed
    itm.setPrice();
    System.out.println("The price is:  $ " + itm.price);
  }
}
```

This program writes the following to the standard output if it compiled and run.

The price was: $ 70.0
The price is: $ 80.0

The method setPrice changes the variable price from $ 70 to $ 80 .

If you need to change the price to other amounts this method is inconvenient. To solve this problem we use parameters.

7.3. Parameters

A parameter could be a primitive variable or an object, and you can pass zero or more parameters to a method. In the example 1, the method getDiscountPrice calculates only the price with a discount of 20%. If we need to calculate different discount rates to our choice, that method doesn't fit our need. To do this more efficiently, we use a parameter. So We need to pass a value of a type double to the method as follows:

double getPrice(double discountPercentage)

Parameters are listed between parentheses.
In the following, you can pass any discount percentage to the method, and the method returns the right discount price.

Example 3

```
class Item
{
  double price = 160.0;

  double getDiscounPrice(double discountPercentage)
  {
    double discount = price * discountPercentage;
    double discountPrice = price - discount;
    return discountPrice;
  }
  public static void main(String[] args)
  {
    Item itm = new Item();
    System.out.println("12%: $" + itm.getDiscounPrice(0.12));
    System.out.println("20%: $" + itm.getDiscounPrice(0.20));
    System.out.println("25%: $" + itm.getDiscounPrice(0.25));
    System.out.println("30%: $" + itm.getDiscounPrice(0.30));
  }
}
```

If the program is compiled and run the following is written to the standard output:

12%: $140.8
20%: $128.0
25%: $120.0
30%: $112.0

In the next method setPrice() you can assign any value you want to the variable price. In this method, we can also pass any price as a parameter to the method.

Example 4

```java
class Item
{
  double price = 70.0;

  /* in the following method you can assign
   * any value to the variable price
   */
  void setPrice(double price)
  {
    this.price = price;
  }
  public static void main(String[] args)
  {
    Item itm = new Item();
    System.out.println("The price was: $" + itm.price);
    itm.setPrice(40.55);
    System.out.println("The price is:  $" + itm.price);
    itm.setPrice(61.35);
    System.out.println("The price is:  $" + itm.price);
    itm.setPrice(54.25);
    System.out.println("The price is:  $" + itm.price);
  }
}
```

If the code is compiled and run the following is written to the standard output.

The price was: $70.0
The price is: $40.55
The price is: $61.35
The price is: $54.25

7.4. A Method With Three Parameters

In the following example the method getSum calculates the sum of three integers and returns the sum as an integer. We can pass any three desired integers we want to the method.

Example 5

```java
class Calculation
{
  int getSum(int number1, int number2, int number3)
  {
    int sum = number1 + number2 + number3;
    return sum;
  }
  public static void main(String[] args)
```

```
{
    Calculation cal = new Calculation();

    System.out.println("17+340+23   = "+cal.getSum(17, 340, 23));
    System.out.println("23+450+353 = "+cal.getSum(23, 450, 353));
    System.out.println("354+12+578 = "+cal.getSum(354, 12, 578));
    System.out.println("37+670+45   = "+cal.getSum(37, 670, 45));
  }
}
```

If the program is compiled and run the following is to the standard output.

```
17 + 340 + 23  = 380
23 + 450 + 353 = 826
354 + 12 + 578 = 944
37 + 670 + 45  = 752
```

7.5. The Variable Sorts

The three sorts variables in Java are Instance variables, local variables and class variables.

7.5.1. Instance variables

An instance variable is declared within a class, but outside of the methods, constructors or other blocks. The instance variables are created when an object is created. They are visible for all methods, constructors, and blocks in the class. Instance variables don't need to be necessarily initialized because they have default values. The default values of the variables are already mentioned in earlier in this book data Types and variables. To access the variables of the object em, use the name of the object and the name of the variable separated by a dot, as shown in example 6.

7.5.2. Local variables

A local variable is a variable that is declared within a method, constructor or a block. Local variables must be initialized because they don't have default values. Local variables are visible only within the method, constructor or block of code in which they are located, such as the variable taxRate in Example 6.

7.5.3. Class variables

Class variables are also called static variables. They are declared inside a class but outside the methods, constructors or blocks. There is only one copy of the class variable available for all the objects. You can get access to a class variable with the name of an object of the class as well as the name of the class separated by a dot, as shown in example 6.

Example 6

The following program writes 3300.0, 300 to the standard output.

```
class Employee
{
    String name; // instance variable
```

```java
double grossSalary = 3300; // instance variable
static int numberEmployees = 300; // class variable

double getNetSalary()
{
   double taxRate = 0.30; // local variable
   double netSalary = grossSalary - (grossSalary * taxRate);
   return netSalary;
}
public static void main(String[] args)
{
   Employee em = new Employee();
   System.out.print(em.grossSalary + ", ");
   System.out.print(Employee.numberEmployees);
}
}
```

7.6. Wrapper classes

Java is an object oriented programming language and treats everything as an object. Primitive variables in Java are not objects. Sometimes it is useful to convert primitive variables to objects, and the other way around. For each primary variable, there is a wrapper class in the Java-library, that has the same name but starts with a capital letter. You sometimes need a wrapper object if a method expects an object as parameter rather than a primitive variable. You can also use methods of the wrapper classes to convert primitive variables to objects or the other way around. You can find out more about Wrapper classes and their methods in Java API-documentation.

Primitive type	Wrapper class
boolean	Boolean
byte	Byte
char	Character
double	Double
float	Float
int	Integer
long	Long
short	Short

Example 7
In the following program the int variable is converted to an Integer object, and the other way around.

```java
class WrapperClass
{
   public static void main(String[] args)
```

```
{
    int i = 23;
    // convert an integer variable to an object
    Integer intObject = new Integer(i);
    // convert an object to an integer variable
    int intVar = intObject.intValue();
  }
}
```

Example 8

In the following program, a String representation of an integer is converted to an int type. We use the wrapper Integer.

```
package book._07_methods.ex._08;

class WrapperClass
{
  public static void main(String[] args)
  {
    String str = "8";
    Integer intObject = Integer.valueOf(str);
    int intVar = intObject.intValue();
    System.out.print(intVar);
  }
}
```

Example 9

Another method to convert a String representation of an integer to an int type.

```
class WrapperClass
{
  public static void main(String[] args)
  {
    String str = "8";
    int intVar = Integer.parseInt(str);
    System.out.print(intVar);
  }
}
```

Quiz 1: Calculate the price of gold/ silver in dollars

What happens when the following program is compiled and run?

```java
class PreciousMetal
{
  double ocGoldPrice = 1300.0; // the price of one ounce of gold
  double ocSilverPrice = 20.0; // the price of one ounce of silver
  boolean isGold = true;

  double getMetalPrice(boolean isGold, int ounce)
  {
    if (isGold)
    {
      return ocGoldPrice * ounce;
    }
    else
    {
      return ocSilverPrice * ounce;
    }
  }
  public static void main(String[] args)
  {
    PreciousMetal pm = new PreciousMetal();
    System.out.print(pm.getMetalPrice(false, 4));
    System.out.print(", ");
    System.out.print(pm.getMetalPrice(true, 2));
  }
}
```

Select the correct answer:
   a) This code writes "20.0, 1300" to the standard output.
   b) This code writes "2600.0, 80.0" to the standard output.
   c) This code writes "80.0, 2600.0" to the standard output.
   d) This code writes "5200.0, 40.0" to the standard output.
   e) This code writes nothing to the standard output.

Explanation

The method getMetalPrice() calculates the price of gold and silver in dollar. If the first parameter is true, that means the metal is gold otherwise it is silver.

The second parameter is the amount of ounces of the metal to be calculated in dollar. The double before the name of the method means that the method returns a data type of double. The first statement mc.getMetalPrice(false, 4) calculates the price of 4 ounces of silver, which is 4 * 20.0 = 80.0. The second statement mc.getMetalPrice(true, 2) calculates the price of 2 ounces of gold, which is 2 * 1300.0 = 2600.0.

The correct answer is c.

Exercises

1. If you know that the price of one ounce of Platinum = $ 936.
2. Add a method to the class called getPlatinumPrice to calculate the price of the amount ounces of Platinum in dollar.
3. Try to test your method whether it returns the price of $ 5148 for 5.5 ounces of Platinum.
4. Test Your method further and find the prices of 4.5 ounces, 6 ounces of Platinum.

Quiz 2: A method that returns an integer data type

What happens when the following program is compiled and run?

```java
class Calculation
{
  int i = 5;
  int i2 = 3;

  int getResult()
  {
    i++;
    if (i <= i2)
    {
      return i * i2;
    }
    else if ((i + i2) >= 9)
    {
      return i + i2 + 5;
    }
    return i * i2 + 3;
  }
  public static void main(String[] args)
  {
    Calculation cal = new Calculation();
    System.out.print(cal.getResult());
  }
}
```

Select the correct answer:
   a) This code writes "13" to the standard output.
   b) This code writes "14" to the standard output.
   c) This code writes "18" to the standard output.
   d) This code writes "21" to the standard output.
   e) This code writes nothing to the standard output.

Explanation

The statement "int getResult()" means that the method returns a data type of integer.

The statement i++; increments the value of i by one.

i = i + 1 = 5 + 1 = 6;

The statement if(i <= i2) is false.

The statement else if((i + i2) >= 9) is true, because 6 + 3 = 9.

The body of the else if statement is executed and a return statement is reached.

The statement returns i + i2 + 5; returns 6 + 3 + 5 = 14;

The correct answer is b.

Exercises

Write a method called calculate that multiplies two integers.

Calculate (22 * 4) using your method, and check out whether the result is 88.

Test your method further for the numbers 9, 12 and 41, 11.

Quiz 3: A method that doesn't return any value

What happens when the following program is compiled and run?

```java
class MyClass
{
    int i = 3;
    int i2 = 8;

    MyClass()
    {
        i += 4;
        i2 += 2;
    }
    void print()
    {
        int x = i + i2;
        System.out.print(x);
    }
    public static void main(String[] args)
    {
        MyClass mc = new MyClass();
        mc.print();
    }
}
```

Select the correct answer:

    a)   This code writes "11" to the standard output.

    b)   This code writes "15" to the standard output.

    c)   This code writes "17" to the standard output.

d) This code writes "6" to the standard output.

e) This code writes nothing to the standard output.

Explanation

By creating a new object, the constructor MyClass() is invoked.

The statement i += 4, increments the value of i by 4.

i = 3 + 4 = 7;

The statement i2 += 2, adds 2 to the initial value of i2.

i2 = 8 + 2 = 10.

The method public void print() does not return any data types because it is of the type of void. The statement mc.print(); invokes the print method.

The body of the method is executed:

The value int x = i + i2 = 7 + 10 = 17;

The statement System.out.print(x); prints the value of x to the standard output.

The correct answer is c.

Exercises

Write a method called "getNetSalary" that calculates net salaries based on gross salaries. Assume that the tax rate is 20%.

Test your method for each of the following gross salaries.

Repeat step 2 for the following gross salaries if tax rate is 30%.

a. $3000

b. $2400

c. $1466

Quiz 4: A method that doesn't return any value

What happens when the following program is compiled and run?

```java
class MyClass
{
  int x = 2;

  void print()
  {
    for (int i = 0; i <= 3; i++)
    {
      if (i < 2)
      {
        x++;
      }
      else
      {
        x += 2;
      }
```

```
    }
    System.out.print(x);
  }
  public static void main(String[] args)
  {
    MyClass mc = new MyClass();
    mc.print();
  }
}
```

Select the correct answer:
  a) This code writes "6" to the standard output.
  b) This code writes "8" to the standard output.
  c) This code writes "10" to the standard output.
  d) This code writes "2" to the standard output.
  e) This code writes nothing to the standard output.

Explanation

The statement for(int i = 0; i <= 3; i ++) indicates that the loop's body is 4 time executed.
The condition if(i < 2) is true for the i values of 0, 1
The initial value of x = 2; Since the condition if(i < 2) is true for two values of i.
x ++; adds one to the value of x.
x ++; adds one more to the value of x.
x = 2 + 2 = 4;
For the values of i = 2 and 3 the else block is executed.
By executing the else block twice.
x += 2;
x += 2;
x = 4 + 2 + 2 = 8

The correct answer is b.

Exercises

Write a simple method called getGreaterNumber that users can pass two numbers to it. The method must write the greater number to the standard output.
If users pass two equal numbers to the method, it should return -1.
Enter the following combinations of two numbers as a parameter to your method to test it.
57, 57
49, 22
7, 89
0, -3

Quiz 5: Writing a method to convert currencies

What happens when the following program is compiled and run?

```java
class Currency
{
  // dollar exchange rate
  double euro = 0.907; // $1 = â,¬ 0.907
  double britishPound = 0.762; // $1 = Â£ 0.762
  double swissFranc = 0.986; // $1 = 0.986 CHF
  double chineseYuan = 6.674; // $1 = Â¥6.674
  double russianRuble = 64.459; // $1 = 64.459 RUB

  void convertToDollar(char currency, int amount)
  {
    switch (currency)
    {
      case ('e'):
        System.out.print(amount * euro);
        break;
      case ('p'):
        System.out.print(amount * britishPound);
        break;
      case ('f'):
        System.out.print(amount * swissFranc);
        break;
      case ('y'):
        System.out.print(amount * chineseYuan);
        break;
      case ('r'):
        System.out.print(amount * russianRuble);
        break;
      default:
        System.out.print("Invalid");
    }
  }
  public static void main(String[] args)
  {
    Currency cr = new Currency();
    cr.convertToDollar('f', 100);
  }
}
```

Select the correct answer:
 a) This code writes "98.6" to the standard output.
 b) This code writes "98.6 Invalid" to the standard output.
 c) This code writes "Invalid" to the standard output.
 d) This code does not compile.
 e) This code writes nothing to the standard output.

Explanation

This method has two parameters.

The first parameter char currence determines the currency type.

The second parameter int amount determines the amount of money you want to convert to US dollar.

We pass 'f' as parameter, which represents Swiss franc.

The statement System.out.print(amount * swissFrank); prints 100 * 0.986 = 98.6 to the standard output.

The break statement terminates the program.

The correct answer is a.

Exercises

1. From the variables, you can conclude that 1 dollar is equal to 0.907 euro and also equal to 6.674 yuan.
2. Write a new method called convertEuroToChineseYuan, the method can convert every amount of euros to yuan.
3. Try to convert the amount of 100 euro to test the method.
4. Try step 2 for the amounts: 220, 300, 2.
5. Compile and run the program to test your method.

Quiz 6: Passing two parameters to a void type method

What happens when the following program is compiled and run?

```java
class MyClass
{
  void myMethod(int x, int y)
  {
    int z = 4;
    int i = 3;
    i++;
    if (x < y)
    {
      z += 4;
    }
    if (x * x > y)
    {
      z += 2;
    }
    else
    {
      z += 6;
    }
    z++;
    System.out.print(z);
  }
}
```

```java
public static void main(String[] args)
{
   MyClass mc = new MyClass();
   mc.myMethod(3, 9);
}
}
```

Select the correct answer:
   a) This code writes "18" to the standard output.
   b) This code writes "16" to the standard output.
   c) This code writes "14" to the standard output.
   d) This code writes "15" to the standard output.
   e) This code writes nothing to the standard output.

Explanation

The initial value of i is 3.

The initial value of z is 4;

The statement if(x < y) is true. z += 4 adds 4 to the initial value of z.

z = 4 + 4 = 8.

The statement if(x * x > y) is false, because 3 * 3 is not greater than 9.

The else body is executed.

The statement z += 6; adds 6 to the value of z.

z = 8 + 6 = 14.

z++; adds one to the value of z.

z = 14 + 1 = 15.

The correct answer is d.

Exercises

Add a new method called getSmallestNumber to the class that print the smallest value of three integer to the standard output. If two or more of the values are equal the method should write 0 to the standard output.

Test your method by passing the set numbers 78, 44, 33, your method should print 33 to the standard output.

Test your method for the following set of numbers:

-2, 3, 0

55, 23, 123

44, 44, 20

34, 34, 34

11, 11, 55

Compile and run the program to test your method.

Assignment: A method that calculates amount ounce of gold

1. Create a new class with the name Gold.
2. Assume that the price of 1 ounce of gold is $ 1300.00.

3. Write the method getOunce in the class Gold . The method provides the amount of ounce of gold for any amount of money that passes through the method.
4. Test your method for the amount of $ 7150, which should return almost 5.5 ounce of gold.
5. Test your method for the amounts $ 1300, $ 2600 and $ 5525.
6. Compile and run the program to test the method.

8. Strings & StringBuffer

8.1. Java API Documentation

There is a rich library of classes and methods available in Java. This huge amount of free source code helps programmers to develop software faster. The documentation of the Java library is online available. For some of the assignments of this book, you will be asked to use this API documentation (Application Programming Interface), because every Java programmer should be able to use this API. String and StringBuffer are both two classes of this Java library.

String class
A string in Java is an object that consists of a random series of characters. A String is enclosed in quotation marks. The String class contains a number of important methods to manipulate it. There are two methods for the declaring of the string object. The most commonly used method is:

String str = "I feel good";

You can also declare a string object in the common way as following.

String str = new String ("I feel good");

Strings cannot be changed once they are created, because they are immutable.

String str = "California";
str = "large";

It seems as if the second line reassigns the value large to the object str, but they are in fact two different objects. Since strings are immutable that makes the process faster.

8.2. Methods of the String class

The String class has a number of useful methods. Below, we describe some of those methods. For more methods and info about strings, see the API documentation.

Method	Return data type	Description
length ()	int	Returns the length of the String.
toUpperCase ()	String	Converts all the characters to uppercase
toLowerCase ()	String	Converts all the characters to lowercase
equals (Object o)	boolean	Returns true if the Strings have the same length and same characters (case sensitive)
charAt (int index)	char	Returns the character at a specific index

indexOf ()	int	Returns the index of the first or last occurrence of a character of substring
substring(int beginIndex, int endIndex)	String	Returns a substring, begins at the specified beginIndex and extends to the character at index endIndex −1. Example: "Hello World".substring(4, 8) returns "llo"
trim()	String	Returns a copy of the String with leading and trailing white space removed
replace(char old, char new)	String	Returns a new string and replaces all the old chars with the new chars

In the following example you learn what you can do with some of the above methods. For more methods and information about strings visit the API documentation.

Example 1

```java
public class MyClass
{
  public static void main(String[] args)
  {
    String text = "If you love what you do, you will never have to work.";
    String text2 = "Julia";
    String text3 = "Julia";
    String text4 = "julia";
    String text5 = "Java #is a #popular programm#ing language.";
    System.out.println("-------------------------------------");
    System.out.println("Number of characters: " + text.length());
    System.out.println("Uppercase: " + text.toUpperCase());
    System.out.println("Small letters: " + text.toLowerCase());
    System.out.println("From 12th to 28th: " + text.substring(12, 30));
    // the index starts with 0
    System.out.println("The seventh character: " + text.charAt(7));
    System.out.println("-------------------------------------");
    System.out.println("is text2 = text3: " + text2.equals(text3));
    // case-sensitive
    System.out.println("is text3 = text4: " + text3.equals(text4));
    System.out.println("-------------------------------------");
    System.out.println("Remove the hash: " + text5.replace("#", ""));
  }
}
```

This program writes the following to the standard output if it is compiled and run.

Number of characters: 53

Uppercase: IF YOU LOVE WHAT YOU DO, YOU WILL NEVER HAVE TO WORK.

Small letters: if you love what you do, you will never have to work.

From 12th to 28th: what you do, you w

The seventh character: l

----

is text2 = text3: true

is text3 = text4: false

Remove the hash: Java is a popular programming language.

Example 2

```
public class MyClass
{
  public static void main(String[] args)
  {
    String str = "his ";
    str += "name ";
    str += "is James.";
    System.out.print(str);
  }
}
```

This program writes his name is James to the standard output.

8.3. StringBuffers

If you need to change a string frequently, it might be better to use StringBuffer. A String is immutable and cannot be changed, but a StringBuffer is changeable. You can instantiate a StringBuffer the same way you instantiate any other objects from a class. The disadvantage of the StringBuffer is that it is slower than the String.

Constructors and Description

StringBuffer()	Creates a StringBuffer with no characters in it with an initial capacity of 16 characters.
StringBuffer(String str)	Creates a StringBuffer initialized to the contents of the specified string.

Method	Return data type	Description
append(int i)	StringBuffer	Appends the string representation of the `int` argument to this sequence.
append(String str)	StringBuffer	Appends the specified string to this character sequence.
delete(int start, int end)	StringBuffer	Removes the characters in a substring of this sequence.
deleteCharAt(int index)	StringBuffer	Removes the `char` at the specified position in this sequence.
insert(int offset, String str)	StringBuffer	Inserts the string into this character sequence.
replace(int start, int end, Strin str)	StringBuffer	Replaces the characters in a substring of this sequence with characters in the specified string.
toString()	String	Returns a string representing the data in this sequence.

In the following example you learn what you can do with some of the above methods. For more methods and information about StringBuffers visit the Java API documentation.

Example 3

```java
public class MyClass
{
  public static void main(String[] args)
  {
    StringBuffer sb = new StringBuffer("The universe is 13.8 billion years");
    sb.append(" old.");
    System.out.println(sb);
    sb.insert(16, "approximately ");
    System.out.println(sb);
    sb.delete(3, 12);
    System.out.println(sb);
  }
}
```

This program writes the following to the standard output if it is compiles and run.

The universe is 13.8 billion years old.
The universe is approximately 13.8 billion years old.
The is approximately 13.8 billion years old.

Quiz 1: Some standard methods of the string object

What happens when the following program is compiled and run?

```java
class Quote
{
  String strQuote = "The weak can never forgive.";

  void myMethod()
  {
    System.out.print(strQuote.charAt(4));
    System.out.print(", " + strQuote.indexOf("k"));
    System.out.print(", " + strQuote.indexOf("e"));
  }
  public static void main(String[] args)
  {
    Quote qt = new Quote();
    qt.myMethod();
  }
}
```

Select the correct answer:
a) This code writes "e, 8, 3" to the standard output.
b) This code writes "w, 7, 0" to the standard output.
c) This code writes "w, 7, 2" to the standard output.
d) This code writes "e, 8, 0" to the standard output.
e) This code writes ", 8, 0" to the standard output.
f) This code writes nothing to the standard output.

Explanation

1. The statement System.out.print(strQuote.charAt(4)); prints the fourth character to the standard output.
2. Starting with 0, the fourth character in the quote is "w".
3. The statement System.out.print(" " + strQuote.indexOf('k')); searches the index of the first character "k" in the text, which is 7 and print it to the standard output.
4. The statement System.out.print(" " + strQuote.indexOf('e')); finds the index of the first "e" in the text.
5. Remember that the text contains several e characters,
6. but the indexOf('e') finds the index of the first one.

The correct answer is c.

Exercises

Declare a string variable and assign the value "I feel good" to it.
Add a statement to write the 7th character from your string.
Add a statement to find the index of the character l.

Quiz 2: Java strings

What happens when the following program is compiled and run?

```java
class MyClass
{
  String str1 = "Jack";
  String str2 = new String("Jack");

  void myMethod()
  {
    if (str1 == str2)
    {
      System.out.print("X");
    }
    if (str1.equals(str2))
    {
      System.out.print("Y");
    }
    else
    {
      System.out.print("Z");
    }
  }
  public static void main(String[] args)
  {
    MyClass mc = new MyClass();
    mc.myMethod();
  }
}
```

Select the correct answer:
a) This code writes "X Z" to the standard output.
b) This code writes "X Y" to the standard output.
c) This code writes "Y" to the standard output.

d) This code writes null to the standard output.

e) This code writes nothing to the standard output.

Explanation

1. The statement if (str1 == str2) returns false because str1 and str2 are two different objects.
2. The statement if(str1.equals(str2) returns true, because both objects contain the same set of chars "Jack".
3. The statement System.out.print("Y"); prints Y to the standard output.
4. The else block is ignored.

The correct answer is c.

Exercises

Write a method that compares two strings. If the content of the strings are equal, the method returns true, otherwise false.

Pass the two strings France and france to your method. Does your method return false or true?

Test your method for the following couple of strings. (Hello, Hello), (123Str, 1234Str) and (He is my friend, He is my friend)

Quiz 3: The substring method

What happens when the following program is compiled and run?

```java
class MyClass
{
  String strQuote = "We cannot solve our problems with the same " +
      "thinking we used when we created them. Albert Einstein";

  void myMethod()
  {
    System.out.println(strQuote.substring(21, 26));
  }
  public static void main(String[] args)
  {
    MyClass mc = new MyClass();
    mc.myMethod();
  }
}
```

Select the correct answer:

a. This code writes "proble" to the standard output.

b. This code writes "problems" to the standard output.

c. This code writes "r prob" to the standard output.

d. This code writes "roble" to the standard output.

e. This code writes nothing to the standard output.

Explanation

The statement strQuote.substring(21,26) returns a substring of the strQuote, which starts from the 21th character to the 26th.

Remember that:

beginIndex - the beginning index, inclusive.

endIndex - the ending index, exclusive.

The correct answer is d.

Exercises
Write a statement that prints the substring "Albert Einstein from strQuote to the standard output. Test your code by compiling and running the program.

Quiz 4: Some standard methods of the string object
What happens when the following program is compiled and run?

```java
class MyClass
{
  String str = "He$llo $World$";

  void myMethod()
  {
    System.out.println(str.replace("$", ""));
  }
  public static void main(String[] args)
  {
    MyClass mk = new MyClass();
    mk.myMethod();
  }
}
```

Select the correct answer:
- a) This code writes "Hello World$" to the standard output.
- b) This code writes "He$llo $World$" to the standard output.
- c) This code writes "Hello $World$" to the standard output.
- d) This code writes "Hello World" to the standard output.

Explanation
The statement System.out.print(strQuote.replace("$","")); replaces all the dollar symbols with nothing or removes them.

The correct answer is d.

Exercises
Write a method that replaces euro (€) symbols from a string with a dollar ($) symbol. Test your method for the following amounts "€ 233, € 12, € 90, € 62".

Quiz 5: Some standard methods of the class String
What happens when the following program is compiled and run?

```java
class MyClass
{
  String str = " the subconscious mind ";

  void myMethod()
  {
```

```java
      int strLength = str.length();
      str = str.toUpperCase();
      str = str.trim();
      System.out.println(strLength + " " + str + " " + str.length());
   }
   public static void main(String[] args)
   {
      MyClass mc = new MyClass();
      mc.myMethod();
   }
}
```

Select the correct answer:
  a) This code writes "23 THE SUBCONSCIOUS MIND 21" to the standard output.
  b) This code writes "23 The subconscious mind 21" to the standard output.
  c) This code writes "23 THE SUBCONSCIOUS MIND 23" to the standard output.
  d) This code writes "21 THE SUBCONSCIOUS MIND 21" to the standard output.

Explanation
  1. The method length(); returns the number of characters of the str object including all the white spaces, which is 23.
  2. The method toUpperCase(); returns a new String with all upper case letters.
  3. The method trim(); returns a new String with leading and trailing white space removed.
  4. That is the reason the last str.length returns 21 because the trim() method removes the leading and the trailing white spaces.

The correct answer is a.

Exercises
Write a method that returns the numbers of character in a string.
Test your method for the following Strings.
a. "What we think, we become." Buddha
b. "Logic will get you from A to B. Imagination will take you everywhere." Albert Einstein

Quiz 6: Some standard methods of the class StringBuffer
What happens when the following program is compiled and run?

```java
class MyClass
{
   StringBuffer sb = new StringBuffer();
   StringBuffer sb2 = new StringBuffer("Jack");

   void myMethod()
   {
      sb.append("Elvis ");
      sb2.append(" Ben");
      sb.append(22);
      System.out.print(sb + ", " + sb2);
   }
   public static void main(String[] args)
   {
      MyClass mc = new MyClass();
```

```
      mc.myMethod();
   }
}
```

Select the correct answer:
a. This code writes "Elvis, Jack Ben" to the standard output.
b. This code writes "Elvis 22, Jack Ben" to the standard output.
c. This code writes ", 22 Ben" to the standard output.
d. This code writes "Elvis, Jack" to the standard output.

Explanation

The statement StringBuffer sb = new StringBuffer(); creates an empty StringBuffer object.
The statement sb.append("Elvis "); adds the string Elvis to the sb object.
The statement sb.append(22); adds the integer 22 to the sb object.
The statement StringBuffer sb2 = new StringBuffer("Jack"); creates a new StringBuffer object contains "Jack".
The statement sb2.append(" Ben"); adds the name Ben to the sb2 object.

The correct answer is b.

Exercises
Add the string " music" to the object sb.
Add the string " 2000" to the object sb2.
Compile and run the program to test your changes.

Quiz 7: Some standard methods of the class StringBuffer

When this program is compiled and run, it should write "He is my friend" to the standard output.

```
class MyClass
{
   StringBuffer sb = new StringBuffer("He is friend.");

   void myMethod()
   {
      // insert the code here
      System.out.print(sb);
   }
   public static void main(String[] args)
   {
      MyClass mc = new MyClass();
      mc.myMethod();
   }
}
```

Which one of the following statements you need to use instead of the comment
"// insert code here"?

a. sb.insert(6,"my ");
b. sb.insert(5,"my ");

c. sb.insert(7,"my");

d. sb.insert(5,"my");

Explanation

The statement sb.insert(6,"my "); inserts the right string "my " to the position of the 6th character of the text.

The correct answer is a.

Exercises

Declare a StringBuffer called sb2, sb2 contains the text "He is from ,,, India".

Write a statement to remove all the commas from the text.

Test your code.

Quiz 8: Some methods of the class StringBuffer

When this program is compiled and run, it should write "He was your friend" to the standard output.

```java
class MyClass
{
  StringBuffer sb = new StringBuffer("He was her friend");

  void myMethod()
  {
    // insert the code here
    System.out.print(sb);
  }
  public static void main(String[] args)
  {
    MyClass mc = new MyClass();
    mc.myMethod();
  }
}
```

Which one of the following statements you need to use instead of the comment "// insert code here"?

a. sb.replace(8,11,"your");

b. sb.replace(6,9,"your");

c. sb.replace(7,10,"your");

d. sb.replace(6,11,"your");

Explanation

The statement sb.replace(7,10,"your"); replaces "her" with the "your" string. For more see Java standard API StringBuffer.

The correct answer is c.

Assignment: Methods of the String class

Use Java standard API and Search for the class String. You can find the link to the Java standard API at the beginning of this book.

The text is: "Brazil $ is $ one $of the largest country in the $ world."

Create a class called TextManipulation.
Write a method called stringDemo, that writes the following to the standard output:
a. The upper case of the text.
b. The lower case of the text.
c. The number of the characters of the text.
d. Writes the text without all the $ symbols.
e. Writes the text without the first 14 characters.
f. The last index of the $ symbol.
g. Replaces the word Brazil with Canada

The result should look like:

Upper case: BRAZIL $ IS $ ONE $OF THE LARGEST COUNTRY IN THE $ WORLD.
Lower case: brazil $ is $ one $of the largest country in the $ world.
Number chars: 57
Remove $: Brazil is one of the largest country in the world.
Remove first 14 chars: one $of the largest country in the $ world.
Return only largest country:largest country
The index of the first $:7
The index of the Last $:49
Replace Brazil:Canada $ is $ one $of the largest country in the $ world.

9. Packages & Access Modifiers

Usually, at the top of a Java class, there is a statement as package java.util.date; Java classes are saved in a file with a ".java" extension. Packages are essentially directories, and they are separated from subdirectories with ".". Java supports the import statement to use classes of other packages as: import java.util.Iterator;

Java supports packages for the following reasons:

1. Packages are helpful by organizing your program.
2. Packages could be reused in other programs.
3. Using packages allow programmers to reuse class names.
4. Packages and access modifiers allow programmers to control access to the classes.

9.1. Access Modifiers

Java supports accessibility of the classes and class members with the following keywords. All group members are accessible from classes in which they exist, regardless of what their keywords are.

9.1.1 Public

A public class or member is accessible from any other classes.

9.1.2. Protected

A protected class or member is accessible from classes of the same package. You can also access protected members of a class in other packages if your class extends that class or use it as a superclass. Subclasses and super classes are covered in the chapter Inheritance.

9.1.3. Package/Default

Package or default modifier does not have a keyword. A package class or member is accessible only from classes and members in the same package.

9.1.4. Private

A private class or member is accessible only from the class where it is defined.

The following table shows the access level of the above access modifiers.

Keyword	Class	Package	Subclass	Outside package
public	Yes	Yes	Yes	Yes
package/default	Yes	Yes	No	No
protected	Yes	Yes	Yes	No
private	Yes	No	No	No

To use a public class from other packages in your own classes, you must import it.

In the chapter Strings and StringBuffers, we have used the classes Strings and StringBuffers in our classes without importing them. The reason is that Strings and StringBuffers are in the package java.lang which is automatically imported in all your classes. If you have a class defined in a different Java package, you cannot use them without importing them.

If you, for example, want to use the class ArrayList in the package java.util, you need to use the following import statement in your class: import java.util.ArrayList; If you need to use many classes in the package java.util, you don't need to import each class separately instead you can use .* at the end of the package. This statement means that you import the whole package: import java.util.*;

Example 1

```
import java.util.ArrayList;

public class MyClass
{
  public static void main()
  {
    ArrayList<String> cars = new ArrayList<String>();

    cars.add("Volvo");
    cars.add("BMW");
    cars.add("Toyota");
  }
}
```

So far we have used only one class in each quiz. From now on you can expect one or more classes in the quizzes.

Quiz 1: Access class members from the same package

What happens when the following program is compiled and run?

ClassB.java
```
public class ClassB
{
  public int w = 1;
  protected int x = 2;
  int y = 3;
  private int z = 4;
}
```

ClassA.java
```
public class ClassA
{
  public static void main(String[] args)
  {
    ClassB cb = new ClassB();
    // System.out.print(cb.w); /* 1 */
    // System.out.print(cb.x); /* 2 */
    // System.out.print(cb.y); /* 3 */
    // System.out.print(cb.z); /* 4 */
  }
```

```
}
```
Which statement(s) are true? Choose all that apply.

  a) If statement 1 is uncommented, the code writes "1" to the standard output.
  b) If statement 2 is uncommented, the code writes "2" to the standard output.
  c) If statement 3 is uncommented, the code writes "3" to the standard output.
  d) If statement 4 is uncommented, the code writes "4" to the standard output.

Explanation

The answers a, b and c are true because both classes are in the same package.

Within the same package, access is allowed to the public, protected and default modifiers.

Answer "d" is incorrect because private members cannot be accessed from other classes.

The correct answers are a, b, c.

Exercises

  1. Declare a character type variable myChar in the class ClassB, the variable myChar shouldn't be accessible through the object cb.
  2. Add a statement to the classA to test whether myChar is accessible.

Quiz 2: Different packages and access modifiers

What happens when the following program is compiled and run?

ClassB.java
```
package package_02;

public class ClassB
{
  public int w = 1;
  protected int x = 2;
  int y = 3;
  private int z = 4;
}
```

ClassA.java
```
package package_01;

import package_02.ClassB;

public class ClassA
{
  public static void main(String[] args)
  {
    ClassB cb = new ClassB();
    // System.out.print(cb.w); /* 1 */
    // System.out.print(cb.x); /* 2 */
    // System.out.print(cb.y); /* 3 */
    // System.out.print(cb.z); /* 4 */
  }
}
```

Which statement(s) are true? Choose all that apply.

a) If statement 1 is uncommented, the code writes "1" to the standard output.
b) If statement 2 is uncommented, the code writes "2" to the standard output.
c) If statement 3 is uncommented, the code writes "3" to the standard output.
d) If statement 4 is uncommented, the code writes "4" to the standard output.

Explanation

1. a is the only correct answer because the variable "w" is defined as public.
2. The variable "x" is protected, and it is in the class ClassB, which is outside the package.
3. That applies to the variables "y" and "z" as well, because their access modifiers are package and private.

The correct answer is a.

Exercises

Declare an integer variable called myInt in the ClassB; the object cb should have access to your variable.
Write a statement in ClassA to check out the accessibility of your variable.
ClassA and ClassB in this example are in two different packages, while in the previous one, they were in the same package.

Analyze the difference between this code and the previous one (qz01).

Quiz 3: Different packages and access modifiers

What happens when the following program is compiled and run?

ClassB.java
```
package package_02;

public class ClassB
{
  public int w = 1;
  protected int x = 2;
  int y = 3;
  private int z = 4;

  public void myMethod()
  {
    System.out.print(w);
    System.out.print(x);
    System.out.print(y);
    System.out.print(z);
  }
}
```

ClassA.java
```java
package package_01;

import package_02.ClassB;

public class ClassA
{
  public static void main(String[] args)
  {
    ClassB cb = new ClassB();
    cb.myMethod();
  }
}
```

Which statement(s) are true? Choose all that apply.
a) This code writes "1234" to the standard output.
b) If you remove the "public" modifier from the ClassB, the code writes "1234" to the standard output.
c) If you remove the "public" modifier from the method myMethod, the code writes "1234" to the standard output.
d) This code does not compile.

Explanation
a. ClassA can access all the public methods of the ClassB.

ClassA can access the private, protected and default members of classB indirectly through the public method myMethod.

b. If you remove the public modifier from the ClassB, you cannot access it anymore from ClassA. Because the two classes are in two different packages.

c. If you remove the public modifier from the method myMethod, you cannot access the method from the ClassA.

Answer d is not correct.

The correct answer is a.

Question
What do you expect if you remove the public keyword from the classB?

Assignment: The classes Date and Student in different packages

1. Create two packages, calendar, and personal_data
2. Create a class called DateInfo inside the package calendar
3. The class DateInfo has only three variables, day (type integer), month (integer), year (integer).
4. The three variables day, month and year, are invisible outside the class DateInfo.
5. Define a constructor for the class DateInfo with three-arguments to initialize the variables day, month and year.
6. Write a method called getDateFormat, that returns a date format example; 19/4/2016 (the method returns a String type for simplification)
7. Create a class called Student inside the package personal_data.
8. The Student class has only two variables, name (type String) and birthDate (type DateInfo).

9. Create two student objects for Isabella and David, Isabella's birthDate is 28/8/1998 and David's birthDate is 13/9/1996

10. Write an extra piece of code to write the names and the birth dates of the two students to the standard output as shown below.

---First Student---
Name: Isabella
Birth date: 28/8/1998
---Second Student---
Name: David
Birth date: 13/9/1996

10. Arrays & Array List

An array is a collection of elements of the same type. The number of the elements of arrays is fixed, and each element has a position in the array. The position of the elements is indicated by an integer value called index, which starts from 0. The number of the elements that can fit in an array is called length. An array in Java is not a primitive data type, but an object.
You define an array as follows:

1. Declare a name for the array.
2. You can create an array object as usual with the keyword new.
3. Specify the data type of the array.
4. Specify the length of the array.
5. Add elements to the array.

See the following example:
Here below we define an array of an integer type data. The size of the array is 7, which indicates that only 7 elements can fit in it.

int [] myArray = new int [7]

The section int [] myArray indicates that the array is of the primitive variable int declared with the name or reference myArray. The square brackets [] indicate that it is a reference to an array. The section new int[7] indicates that a new array object is created. The number between the square brackets means that the length of the array is equal to 7. The index of the elements of myArray consists of the numbers 0, 1, 2, 3, 4, 5 and 6. There are seven elements totally. To find out the element for example at index 2, we use the name of the array, and between square brackets the index of the element: myArray[2]. In our example, all the seven elements are equal to 0, because they are not initialized. If an int type variable is not initialized its value is by default equal to 0.
The program of example 1 writes seven zeros to the standard output: 0000000

int [] myArray = new int [7]

The following code changes the value of the fourth element in the array to 11. Remember that the first element index is 0.

intArray [3] = 11

Try to import the package java.util.Arrays of the Java standard API, to learn how to sort the elements of an array. See the standard methods of java.util.Arrays to learn what you can do with the elements of arrays.

Example 1
```
public class MyClass
{
  public static void main(String[] args)
  {
    int[] myArray = new int[7];
```

```
      System.out.print(myArray[0]);
      System.out.print(myArray[1]);
      System.out.print(myArray[2]);
      System.out.print(myArray[3]);
      System.out.print(myArray[4]);
      System.out.print(myArray[5]);
      System.out.print(myArray[6]);
   }
}
```

You can assign other values to the elements of myArray. In the next example we assign new values of 7, 4 and 1 to the elements at index 0, 3, 5 as follows.

myArray[0]   =   7;
myArray[3]   =   4;
myArray[5] = 1;

The following program writes 7004010 to the standard output, because we reassigned the values of the element indexes 0, 3 and 5, to the new values of 7, 4 and 1.

Example 2
```
public class MyClass
{
   public static void main(String[] args)
   {
      int[] myArray = new int[7];
      myArray[0] = 7;
      myArray[3] = 4;
      myArray[5] = 1;

      System.out.print(myArray[0]);
      System.out.print(myArray[1]);
      System.out.print(myArray[2]);
      System.out.print(myArray[3]);
      System.out.print(myArray[4]);
      System.out.print(myArray[5]);
      System.out.print(myArray[6]);
   }
}
```

The array myArray has only seven elements, therefore it was not difficult to write each element value separately to the standard output. If you have an array of hundreds of elements, it would not be practical to use the previous method. To write each element value of that kind of arrays to the standard output, we can use a loop statement such as a for-statement as follows.

Example 3
```
public class MyClass
{
   public static void main(String[] args)
   {
      int[] myArray = new int[7];

      myArray[0] = 7;
```

```
      myArray[3] = 4;
      myArray[5] = 1;

      for (int i = 0; i < myArray.length; i++)
      {
        System.out.print(myArray[i]);
      }
    }
}
```

This program writes 7004010 to the standard output if it is compiled and run.

10.1. Sorting the elements of an array

To sort elements of an array, we use the class Arrays. This class is located in the package java.util of the Java standard API. Below is what you can do with some methods of the class java.util.Arrays.

Methods of Arrays (See Java standard API for more details)

Method	Return data type	Description
sort(Object [] o)	void	Sorts the specified array
copyOf (char[] original, int newLength)	void	Copies the specified array
binarySearch(char[] c, char key)	void	Searches the specified array chars for a specific value.
equals(char[] c, char[] c2)	boolean	Returns true if the two specified arrays of chars are equal.

In the following program we sort the elements of an array

Example 4

```
import java.util.Arrays;

public class MyClass
{
  public static void main(String[] args)
  {
    String[] strArray = new String[5];

    strArray[0] = "Nora";
    strArray[1] = "Sam";
    strArray[2] = "Anna";
    strArray[3] = "Lisa";
    strArray[4] = "Julian";

    System.out.println("The names are not sorted alphabetically.");

    for (int i = 0; i < strArray.length; i++)
    {
      System.out.print(strArray[i] + ", ");
    }
    // the sort method sorts the names alphabetically
```

```java
    Arrays.sort(strArray);
    System.out.println("\n---------");
    System.out.println("The names are sorted alphabetically.");

    for (int i = 0;  i < strArray.length;  i++)
    {
      System.out.print(strArray[i] + ", ");
    }
  }
}
```

When this program is compiled and run, the following is written to the standard output.

The names are not sorted alphabetically.
Nora, Sam, Anna, Lisa, Julian,

The names are sorted alphabetically.
Anna, Julian, Lisa, Nora, Sam,

There is a faster method to define an array and add elements to it.

String[] strArray = {"Nora","Sam","Anna","Lisa","Julian"};
The previous method can replace the following method.
String[] strArray = new String[5];
strArray[0] = "Nora";
strArray[1] = "Sam";
strArray[2] = "Anna";
strArray[3] = "Lisa";
strArray[4] = "Julian";

Example 5

```java
import java.util.Arrays;

public class MyClass
{
  public static void main(String[] args)
  {
    // second method
    String[] strArray = { "Nora", "Sam", "Anna", "Lisa", "Julian" };
    System.out.println("The names are not sorted alphabetically.");

    for (int i = 0;  i < strArray.length;  i++)
    {
      System.out.print(strArray[i] + ", ");
    }
    // the sort method sorts the names alphabetically
    Arrays.sort(strArray);
    System.out.println("\n---------");
    System.out.println("The names are sorted alphabetically.");

    for (int i = 0;  i < strArray.length;  i++)
    {
      System.out.print(strArray[i] + ", ");
```

```
        }
      }
}
```

The code of example 5 writes the following to the standard output.

The names are not sorted alphabetically.
Nora, Sam, Anna, Lisa, Julian,

The names are sorted alphabetically.
Anna, Julian, Lisa, Nora, Sam,

The element strArray[i] is a String object in the index position i . In the chapter Strings and StringBuffer is explained how you can access the methods of objects. To find the number of characters of each String, we can use the method length() as follows:

strArray[i].length()

Example 6

```java
public class MyClass
{
  public static void main(String[] args)
  {
    String[] strArray = new String[5];

    strArray[0] = "Nora";
    strArray[1] = "Sam";
    strArray[2] = "Anna";
    strArray[3] = "Lisa";
    strArray[4] = "Julian";

    System.out.println("The number of characters of the names.");
    for (int i = 0; i < strArray.length; i++)
    {
      System.out.print(strArray[i] + ":"+strArray[i].length()+",");
    }
  }
}
```

The number of characters of the names.
Nora:4,Sam:3,Anna:4,Lisa:4,Julian:6,

10.2. The Class Arraylist

An ArrayList is a data structure that allows you to collect elements in a list. An ArrayList is often used because it's size can change. It is one of the classes in the Java library, which contains different methods to add, remove, sort elements in alphabetical order and more. Each element of an ArrayList has an index which starts from 0. To use an ArrayList in your own classes, you need to import it from the Java library as shown below.

import java.util.ArrayList;

Some Methods of ArrayList (see ArrayList in the Java standard API)

Method	Return data type	Description
add(int index, E element)	void	Inserts an element at a specified position in the list.
add(E element)	boolean	Appends the specified element to the end of the list.
get(int index)	Element	Returns the element at a specified position.
remove(int index)	Element	Removes the element at the specified position
size()	int	Returns the number of elements in the list.

Example 7

```java
import java.util.ArrayList;

public class MyClass
{
   public static void main(String[] args)
   {
      ArrayList arrayList = new ArrayList();
   }
}
```

Quiz 1: A simple array

What happens when the following program is compiled and run?

```java
public class MyArray
{
   public static void main(String[] args)
   {
      int[] arrayInt = new int[3];

      for (int i = 0; i < arrayInt.length; i++)
      {
         System.out.print(arrayInt[i] + " ");
      }
   }
}
```

Select the correct answer:

    a)   This code writes "0 0" to the standard output.

    b)   This code writes "0 0 0" to the standard output.

    c)   This code writes "0" to the standard output.

    d)   This code writes null to the standard output.

    e)   This code writes nothing to the standard output.

Explanation

The statement int[] arrayInt = new int[3]; creates an array of integer.

the new int[3] means that the array length is 3 and only three elements fit in it.

The statement System.out.print(arrayInt[i] + " "); prints the elements of the array to the standard output.

The value of each element of an array is automatically set to a default value. In this case is a default value of an integer, which is 0.

The correct answer is b.

Exercises

Change the declaration of the array to "int[] arrayInt = new int[11];". What would be the result? Compile and run the program to test your expectation.

Quiz 2: Adding integer elements to an Array

What happens when the following program is compiled and run?

```java
public class MyArray
{
    public static void main(String[] args)
    {
        int[] arr = new int[5];

        arr[0] = 3;
        arr[1] = 7;
        arr[4] = 3;
        arr[3] = 1;
        arr[1] = 8;

        for (int i = 0; i < arr.length; i++)
        {
            System.out.print(arr[i] + " ");
        }
    }
}
```

Select the correct answer:

a. This code writes "3 8 7 1 3" to the standard output.

b. This code writes "3 7 0 1 3" to the standard output.

c. This code writes "3 7 1 3 8" to the standard output.

d. This code writes "3 7 3 1 8" to the standard output.

e. This code writes "3 8 0 1 3" to the standard output.

Explanation

The statement int[] arr = new int[5]; creates an array of integer with 5 places.

The statement arr[0] = 3; assigns the value of the first (index = 0) element to 3.

The statement arr[1] = 7; sets the value of the second element to 7.

The statement arr[1] = 8; reassigns the value of the second element to 8.

The third element is not assigned, the default value is 0.

The statement arr[3] = 1; sets the fourth element to 1.

The statement arr[4] = 3; sets the fifth element to 3.

The correct answer is e.

Exercises

In the above program, we want to write to the standard output only the elements that are greater or equal to 3, add your control to achieve that.

compile and run the code to test your expectation.

Quiz 3: Sorting elements of an array

What happens when the following program is compiled and run?

```java
import java.util.Arrays;

public class Animal
{
  public static void main(String[] args)
  {
    String[] arrAnimal = new String[5];

    arrAnimal[0] = "Wolf ";
    arrAnimal[1] = "Lion ";
    arrAnimal[2] = "Leopard ";
    arrAnimal[3] = "Elephant ";
    arrAnimal[4] = "Tiger ";
    // See the class "Arrays" of the Java standard API
    Arrays.sort(arrAnimal);

    for (int i = 0; i < arrAnimal.length; i++)
    {
      if (i > 1)
      {
        System.out.print(arrAnimal[i]);
      }
    }
  }
}
```

Select the correct answer:

a. This code writes "Lion Tiger Wolf" to the standard output.

b. This code writes "Leopard Elephant Tiger" to the standard output.

c. This code writes "Elephant Leopard Lion Tiger Wolf" to the standard output.

d. This code writes "Leopard Lion Tiger Wolf" to the standard output.

e. This code writes "null" to the standard output.

Explanation

The Arrays.sort(arrAnimal); statement sorts the names alphabetically as following.

Elephant, Leopard, Lion, Tiger, Wolf

The statement if(i > 1) prints only the element indexes greater than 1, which are:

Lion, Tiger, Wolf

The correct answer is a.

Exercises

Add three more animals to the arrAnimal namely, Bear, Zebra, and Monkey, in the positions 5, 6 and 7.
By compiling and running the program, the error "java.lang.ArrayIndexOutOfBoundsException" would
be written to the standard output. Try to fix the error.
Change the program so that you print all the elements of the array to the standard output.

Quiz 4: Copying a Java array and sorting its elements

What happens when the following program is compiled and run?

```
import java.util.Arrays;

public class MyArray
{
  public static void main(String[] args)
  {
    char[] arrCharA = new char[4];

    arrCharA[0] = 'g';
    arrCharA[1] = 'h';
    arrCharA[2] = 'e';
    arrCharA[3] = 'f';
    // see the class "Arrays" of the Java standard API
    char[] arrCharB = Arrays.copyOf(arrCharA, arrCharA.length);
    Arrays.sort(arrCharA);

    System.out.print(arrCharA[2]);
    System.out.print(arrCharB[3]);
  }
}
```

Select the correct answer:
a. This code writes "he" to the standard output.
b. This code writes "ef" to the standard output.
c. This code writes "gf" to the standard output.
d. This code writes "ee" to the standard output.
e. This code writes null to the standard output.
f. This code writes nothing to the standard output.
g. This code does not compile.

Explanation

The statement char[] arrCharA = new char[4]; creates an array of char.
The statement char[] arrCharB = Arrays.copyOf(arrCharA,arrCharA.length); copies the array with all its
elements.
The statement Arrays.sort(arrCharA); sorts the original arrCharA.
The elements of the arrCharA are indexed as: e f g h
The elements of the array copy arrCharB are indexed as g h e f.
The statement System.out.print(arrCharA[2]); prints the third element(g) of the arrCharA to the standard
output.
The statement System.out.print(arrCharB[3]); prints the fourth element(f) of the arrCharB to the standard
output.

The correct answer is c.

Exercises

Declare a new array of integers called "arrayInt" and add the elements 3, 4, 2, 7 and 9 to it.

Add a piece of code to write all the values of the elements of your array to the standard output.

Quiz 5: Using methods of the class Arrays

What happens when the following program is compiled and run?

```java
import java.util.Arrays;

public class MyArray
{
  public static void main(String[] args)
  {
    char[] arrCharA = new char[4];

    arrCharA[0] = 'w';
    arrCharA[1] = 'k';
    arrCharA[2] = 'd';
    arrCharA[3] = 'r';

    char[] arrCharB = Arrays.copyOf(arrCharA, arrCharA.length);
    // returns the index of the element 'k'
    int i = Arrays.binarySearch(arrCharA, 'k');
    // checks whether the two arrays are equal
    boolean b = Arrays.equals(arrCharA, arrCharB);
    System.out.print(i + " " + b);
  }
}
```

Select the correct answer:

a. This code writes "0 false" to the standard output.

b. This code writes "0 true" to the standard output.

c. This code writes "1 false" to the standard output.

d. This code writes "1 true" to the standard output.

e. This code does not compile.

Explanation

The statement char[] arrCharB = arrCharA.clone(); clones the arrCharA.

The statement int i = Arrays.binarySearch(arrCharA,'k'); returns the index of the 'k', see Java API.

The index of 'k' is 1.

The statement boolean b = Arrays.equals(arrCharA,arrCharB); returns true if the two arrays are equal otherwise false, see Java API

ArrayB is a clone of ArrayA, and that is why the method equals returns true.

The correct answer is d.

Exercises

Declare an array of character called arrayChar add the elements R, N, B, S, M, O, A and C to it.

Check out whether your array (arrayChar) is equal to the array "arrCharA".

Sort the elements of your array alphabetically, use the "Arrays" class of the Java standard api, import java.util.Arrays; .

Add a piece of code to write the elements of your array to the standard output.

The result should look like: A, B, C, M, N, O, R, S,

Quiz 6: Array elements & conditional statements

What happens when the following program is compiled and run?

```java
public class MyClass
{
  void myMethod()
  {
    String strArray[] = { "n", "b", "a", "z" };

    for (int i = 0; i < strArray.length; i++)
    {
      if (strArray[i].equals("z"))
      {
        System.out.print("x1 ");
      }
      else if (strArray[i].equals("a"))
      {
        System.out.print("x2 ");
      }
      else if (strArray[i].equals("B"))
      {
        System.out.print("x2 ");
      }
      else
      {
        System.out.print("x3 ");
      }
    }
  }
  public static void main(String[] args)
  {
    MyClass mc = new MyClass();
    mc.myMethod();
  }
}
```

Select the correct answer:

a. This code writes "x3 x2 x2 x1" to the standard output.

b. This code writes "x3 x3 x3 x3" to the standard output.

c. This code writes "x1 x2 x3 x3" to the standard output.

d. This code writes "x3 x3 x2 x1" to the standard output.

e. This code does not compile.

Explanation

When "i" is equal to 0, the if statements, checks whether the first element of the array is z, a or B.

The first element of the array is "n", and that is why x3 is printed to the standard output.

The second element of the array is "B", which is no equal to small "b", x3 is printed to the standard output.

The third element is equal to "a", and that is why x2 is printed to the standard output.

The fourth element is z, and that is why x1 is printed to the standard output.

The correct answer is d.

Exercises

What is written to the standard output if the statement else if(strArray[i].equals("B")) is replaced by the statement else if(strArray[i].equals("b")) .

Compile and run the program to check.

Quiz 7: Add and retrieve elements from an ArrayList

What happens when the following program is compiled and run?

```java
import java.util.ArrayList;

public class CountryList
{
  public static void main(String[] args)
  {
    ArrayList<String> counties = new ArrayList<String>();

    counties.add("Germany");
    counties.add("United States");
    counties.add("Russia");
    counties.add("United Kingdom");
    counties.add(2, "India");

    for (int i = 0; i < counties.size(); i++)
    {
      System.out.print(" " + counties.get(i));
    }
  }
}
```

Select the correct answer:
  a) This code writes "Germany United States Russia United Kingdom" to the standard output.
  b) This code writes "Germany India United States Russia United Kingdom" to the standard output.
  c) This code writes "Germany United States Russia United Kingdom India" to the standard output.
  d) This code writes "Germany United States India Russia United Kingdom" to the standard output.

You can find the link to the Java standard API at the beginning of this book. Write a method called printInfo that writes the following to the standard output.

Explanation

The program inserts India at the second index position in the list. Since the index of an ArrayList starts with 0.

The position of India will be the third position in the list.

The correct answer is d.

Exercises
Use Java standard API and search for the class ArrayList.

Check whether the ArrayList countries is empty.
Check whether "Spain" is on the list.
Check whether "Russia" is on the list.
The index of the United States.
The size of the ArrayList countries.
Remove Germany from the list.

Quiz 8: Add and retrieve elements from a student ArrayList

What happens when the following program is compiled and run?

Student.java
```java
public class Student
{
  String name;
  int age;
  String email;

  public Student(String name, int age, String email)
  {
    this.name = name;
    this.age = age;
    this.email = email;
  }
}
```

College.java
```java
import java.util.ArrayList;

public class College
{
  ArrayList<Student> studentList = new ArrayList<Student>();

  public void populateStudentArray()
  {
    Student st1 = new Student(" Smith", 24, "smith@itmail.com");
    Student st2 = new Student(" Jennifer", 22, "jennifer@dzork.com");
    Student st3 = new Student(" Thomas", 33, "thomas@ysmail.com");
    Student st4 = new Student(" Susan", 25, "susan@rzmail.com");

    studentList.add(st1);
    studentList.add(st2);
    studentList.add(st3);
    studentList.add(st4);
  }
  public static void main(String[] args)
```

```java
{
  College cl = new College();
  cl.populateStudentArray();

  for (int i = 0; i < cl.studentList.size(); i++)
  {
    if (i == 2)
    {
      System.out.print(cl.studentList.get(i).name +
          ", " + cl.studentList.get(i).age +
          ", " + cl.studentList.get(i).email);
    }
  }
}
}
```

a. This code writes "Jennifer, 22, jennifer@dzork.com" to the standard output.

b. This code writes "Susan, 25, susan@rzmail.com" to the standard output.

c. This code writes "Thomas, 33, thomas@ysmail.com" to the standard output.

d. This code writes "Smith, 24, smith@itmail.com" to the standard output.

Explanation

If you remove the statement "if(i == 2)", the program retrieves all the four students names and emails.
The previous statement selects only the second student. Since the ArrayList index starts from 0.
The information about the third student(Thomas) is printed to the standard output.
We added four elements to the ArrayList, and that means the size of the ArrayList is 4.

The correct answer is c.

Exercises

Add another student to the list, whose name is "Rita", age 28 and her email is "rita@online.com".
What is the result if you remove the conditional statement "if(i == 2)" ?
What is the result if you remove the statement "cl.populateSutdentArray();"
Compile and run the program to test your expectation.

Assignment: Add items to a shopping cart

1. Create a new class named Item. Declare two variables within this class, namely, name and price .
2. Define a constructor for the class Item to initialize the names and the prices of the items.
3. Create a class shopping Cart with an object ArrayList for the items.
4. Add the following items to the ArrayList.

Shirt price $ 20.39

Pants price $ 32.85

Socks price $ 11.25

Jacket price $ 120.65

Write a method with the name printItems to write the names and the prices of the items to the standard output.

11. Static Members

Static members are variables, methods, or nested classes, the last one will be explained later in this book. All objects have their own copy of the instance variables, but for the static variable, there is only one copy available for all the objects of the class. You can call static variables with the name of the class as well as the name of each instance of the class. A static variable is also called class variable; it starts with the keyword static.

11.1. Class Variables

In the following class Student, we want to keep track of the numbers of objects we instantiate from the class student. To do this, we need to declare a static int variable numberStudents. Each time you instantiate a student object, the constructor increments the number of students by one. In the following program, three objects are created, namely st1, st2 and st3.

Example 1

```java
public class Student
{
  String name;
  static int numberStudents;

  public Student()
  {
    numberStudents++;
  }
  public static void main(String[] args)
  {
    Student st1 = new Student();
    Student st2 = new Student();
    Student st3 = new Student();

    st1.name = "Allan";
    st2.name = "Erica";
    st3.name = "Emma";

    System.out.println("Name st1: " + st1.name);
    System.out.println("Number of students: " + st1.numberStudents);
    System.out.println("Name st2: " + st2.name);
    System.out.println("Number of students: " + st2.numberStudents);
    System.out.println("Name st3: " + st3.name);
    System.out.println("Number of students: "+st3.numberStudents);
    /*
     * you can access static variables by using the Name of the class
     */
    System.out.println("Number of students: "+Student.numberStudents);
```

```
      }
}
```

The previous example writes the following to the standard output.

Name st1: Allan
Number of students: 3
Name st2: Erica
Number of students: 3
Name st3: Emma
Number of students: 3
Number of students: 3

This kind of information cannot be provided by the instance variables because each object has information about itself. Objects have no information about the history of their classes. If we remove the keyword static from the variable numberStudents the number of students remains 1, regardless of the number of objects that you create.

How to prevent instantiation of a class with only static members?
It is unnecessary to instantiate classes that have only static variables and methods such as the Math class of the Java standard API. To prevent instantiating such a class you need to define its constructor private.

11.2. Static Methods

You can call static members with the name of the class, and that also applies to the static methods. You can call static methods with the name of the class as well as the name of the objects.
There are some important rules, which apply to static methods.

The keyword this can't be used inside static methods because this is associated with the current instance. You can not have instance variables within a static method because the instance probably does not exist at the time that the method is called.

An example of a static method is the following method, which returns the sum of four integers. This method is static because there is no need to create an object to calculate the sum of four integers. In order to call this method, we use the name of the class.

Example 2
```
public class Calculate
{
  public static int getSum(int i, int i2, int i3, int i4)
  {
    return i + i2 + i3 + i4;
  }
  public static void main(String[] args)
  {
    int x = getSum(5, 4, 6, 2);
```

```
  // or
  // int x = Calculate.getSum(5, 4, 6, 2);
  System.out.print(x);
  }
}
```

The previous example writes 17 to the standard output.

Quiz 1: Comparing static variables with instance variables

What happens when the following program is compiled and run?

```
public class Employee
{
  int nr; // instance variable
  static int stNr; // class variable

  public Employee()
  {
    nr++;
    stNr++;
  }
  public static void main(String[] args)
  {
    Employee emp1 = new Employee();
    Employee emp2 = new Employee();
    Employee emp3 = new Employee();

    System.out.print(Employee.stNr + ", ");
    System.out.print(emp1.nr + ", ");
    System.out.print(emp2.nr + ", ");
    System.out.print(emp3.nr);
  }
}
```

Select the correct answer:
a. This code writes "3, 1, 2, 3" to the standard output.
b. This code writes "3, 1, 1, 1" to the standard output.
c. This code writes "1, 1, 1, 1" to the standard output.
d. This code writes "3, 3, 3, 3" to the standard output.
e. This code writes nothing to the standard output.

Explanation
The no-argument constructor is called each time we create an employee object.

We have created 3 employee objects and by creating an object the statement stNr++ adds one to the static variable. After creating the three objects stNr = 3.

For all the instances the stNr remains the same because it is static.

Usually, you don't need to use the name of objects to access static members. You can also use the name of the class.

The instance variable nr belongs to the objects. The value of the instance variable nr for all the objects is equal to one.

The correct answer is b.

Exercises

Create two more employee objects namely; emp4 and emp5.

Does the instantiation of the two previous objects affect the static variable stNr?

Compile and run the program to test your expectation.

Quiz 2: Java static members

What happens when the following program is compiled and run?

```java
public class MyClass
{
   static int x = 3;

   public MyClass()
   {
     x++;
   }
   public static int method(int i, int i2)
   {
     x += (i - i2);
     return x;
   }
   public static void main(String[] args)
   {
     MyClass mc1 = new MyClass();
     MyClass mc2 = new MyClass();
     System.out.print(MyClass.x + ", ");
     MyClass mc3 = new MyClass();
     MyClass.method(8, 3);
     System.out.print(MyClass.x);
   }
}
```

Select the correct answer:

a. This code writes "0, 0" to the standard output.

b. This code writes "5, 5" to the standard output.

c. This code writes "11, 11" to the standard output.

d. This code writes "5, 11" to the standard output.

e. This code writes "3, 3" to the standard output.

Explanation

The no-argument constructor is called each time we create a MyClass object.

By instantiating the objects mc1 and mc2 the no-argument constructor adds each time 1 to the value of x which is initially equal to 3.

$x = 3 + 1 + 1 = 5$.

By instantiating the object mc3 the no-argument constructor adds one more to the value of x.

$x = 5 + 1 = 6$.

The statement MyClass.method(8,3); invokes the method, which adds (i - i2) to the value of x.

$x = 6 + (8 - 3) = 11$.

The correct answer is d.

Exercises

Write a method called resetX to reset the value of the variable x to any integer number you wish. Test your method.

Quiz 3: Class variables and instance variables

What happens when the following program is compiled and run?

```java
public class MyClass
{
  static int x = 6;
  int y = 3;

  MyClass()
  {
    x += 3;
    y += 2;
  }
  void method(int i)
  {
    this.y = y - i;
    x++;
  }
  public static void main(String[] args)
  {
    MyClass mc1 = new MyClass();
    MyClass mc2 = new MyClass();
    MyClass mc3 = new MyClass();
    mc1.method(3);
```

```
        System.out.print(MyClass.x + ", " + mc1.y);
    }
}
```

Select the correct answer:

a. This code writes "16, 6" to the standard output.

b. This code writes "16, 2" to the standard output.

c. This code writes "12, 2" to the standard output.

d. This code writes "13, 5" to the standard output.

e. This code writes "15, 5" to the standard output.

Explanation

1. The statement MyClass mc1 = new MyClass(); creates the object mc1.
2. By creating an object, the program calls the no-argument constructor.
3. It adds 3 to the value of x and 2 to the value of y.
4. x = 6 + 3 = 9. x is static and it belongs to the class.
5. y = 3 = 2 = 5. y is an instance variable and its value belongs to the object mc1.
6. The statement MyClass mc2 = new MyClass(); creates the object mc2.
7. It calls the no-argument constructor and adds more 3 to the value of x.
8. x = 9 + 3 =12. The value of y of the object mc1 remains the same.
9. The statement MyClass mc3 = new MyClass(); creates the object mc3.
10. It calls the no-argument constructor and adds more 3 to the value of x.
11. x = 12 + 3 = 15.
12. The statement mc1.method(3); invokes the method, which adds one to the value of x.
13. x = 15 + 1 = 16.
14. By invoking the method
    this.y = (y - i)
15. The value of the variable y of the object mc1 is equal to 5.
    y = 5 - i = 5 - 3 = 2.

The correct answer is b.

Exercises

Create five object references of the class MyClass namely mc4, mc5, mc6, mc7 and mc8.

Does that affect the static variable x?

Test your code.

Quiz 4: Static variables and methods

What happens when the following program is compiled and run?

```
public class MyClass
{
    static int x = 2;

    MyClass()
```

```java
    {
      x += 4;
    }
    static void methodA(int i)
    {
      x = x - i;
    }
    int methodB(int i)
    {
      return x + i;
    }
    public static void main(String[] args)
    {
      MyClass mc1 = new MyClass();
      MyClass.methodA(2);
      MyClass mc2 = new MyClass();
      System.out.print(mc2.methodB(3));
    }
}
```

Select the correct answer:

a. This code writes "11" to the standard output.

b. This code writes "12" to the standard output.

c. This code writes "14" to the standard output.

d. This code writes "7" to the standard output.

e. This code writes "9" to the standard output.

Explanation

1. The statement MyClass mc1 = new MyClass(); calls the no-argument constructor, which adds 4 to the value of x.
2. x = 2 + 4 = 6.
3. The statement MyClass.methodA(2); invokes the methodA.
4. x = x - i = 6 - 2 = 4.
5. The statement MyClass mc2 = new MyClass(); calls the no-argument constructor, which adds 4 to the value of x.
6. x = 4 + 4 = 8.
7. The statement System.out.print(mc2.methodB(3)); invokes the methodB.
8. x = x + i = 8 + 3 = 11.

The correct answer is a.

Exercises

What is the result if you replace the statement x += 4; with the statement x ++

Compile and run the program to test the result.

Quiz 5: A static StringBuffer example

What happens when the following program is compiled and run?

public class MyClass
{
  static int *x*;
  static StringBuffer *sb* = **new** StringBuffer();

```
public class MyClass
{
    static int x;
    static StringBuffer sb = new StringBuffer();

    public MyClass()
    {
        myMethod();
    }
    public void myMethod()
    {
        x += 3;
        sb.append(x);
    }
    public static void main(String[] args)
    {
        MyClass mc = new MyClass();
        MyClass mc2 = new MyClass();
        MyClass mc3 = new MyClass();
        System.out.println(MyClass.sb);
    }
}
```

Select the correct answer:
a. This code writes "333" to the standard output.
b. This code writes "0" to the standard output.
c. This code writes "3" to the standard output.
d. This code writes "369" to the standard output.
e. This code writes "18" to the standard output.

Explanation

1. The statement MyClass mc = new MyClass(), creates an object, which calls the MyClass no-argument constructor.
2. The constructor invokes the method myMethod().
3. The statement x += 3 increments the value of x by 3, x = 0 + 3 = 3.
4. The statement sb.appends(x), appends the string representation of the x argument, which is 3.

5. By creating the second object "mc2" the x += 3 increments the value of x by 3, x = 3 + 3 = 6.
6. The statement sb.appends(x), appends the string representation of the x argument, which is 6.

7. By creating the third object "mc3" the x += 3 increments the value of x by 3, x = 6 + 3 = 9.
8. The statement sb.appends(x), appends the string representation of the x argument, which is 9.

9. Remember that x and sb are both static, and that is why both of them belong to the class. The value of x and sb are the same for all the objects.

The correct answer is d.

Exercises
Remove the keyword static from the class variable x .
Does the previous step affect the program?
Compile and run the program to check your expectation.
Remove both static keywords from the class variables x and sb .
Do you think that the previous step changes the result of the execution of the program?
Compile and run the program to check your expectation.

Assignment: Track the names of programming languages in a string

1. Create a new class ProgrammingLanguage.
2. Declare an integer variable numberOfLanguages and a String variable language inside the class.
3. Instantiate the following five objects of the class ProgrammingLanguage as follows: Java , C++ , Python , PHP and Ruby .
4. Each time an object is created, the variable language keeps the track of the name of the objects as follows: Java , C++ , Python , PHP , Ruby .
5. The variable numberOfLanguages should also keep track the number of the created objects.
6. Compile and run your program to test your code.

Use the operator += to keep track of the variable language of all the created objects, as follows :
String language = "".
language += "Java".
language += "C++".. etc.

12. Inheritance

Java supports inheritance to allow reusing code and extending new classes based on existing ones. Inheritance is an important concept in object-oriented programming.

An example of inheritance is an Employee class, which contains the fields, name, age, and salary. If we need to know which programming language a programmer use, we cannot add that field to the employee class. That is because not every employee works with a programming language. The mentioned field would be redundant for the managers and other employees, who are not programmers.

Example 1

```java
public class Employee
{
  String name;
  int age;
  double salary;
  String language; // redundant

  public void printInfo()
  {
    System.out.println("Name:       " + name);
    System.out.println("Age:        " + age);
    System.out.println("Salary $    " + salary);
    System.out.println("Language:   " + language);
  }
}
```

Another solution is creating a new class called programmer with the fields name , age , salary and language as following. In the following

```java
public class Programmer
{
  String name; // redundant
  int age; // redundant
  double salary; // redundant
  String language;

  public void printInfo()
  {
    System.out.println("Name:       " + name);
    System.out.println("Age:        " + age);
    System.out.println("Salary:     " + salary);
    System.out.println("Language:   " + language);
  }
}
```

This solution also uses unnecessary fields, because we have already defined the fields name, age, and salary in the class Employee. To reuse the code of the class Employee, we will extend the class Programmer with the keyword extends. In this way, the class Programmer inherits all the fields and the behaviors of the class Employee.

The class Programmer inherits the fields name, age, and salary from the class Employee and keeps its own field language. The term superclass is used for the parent class and the term subclass for the child class. In our example, the class Programmer becomes a subclass of the superclass Employee as shown in example 2. The keyword protected is used for the members of the superclass to give the subclass access to those members.

The method printInfo in the class Employee writes the name, age, and salary of the employees to the standard output. We can override this method in the class Programmer to write those attributes of each programmer in addition to the programming language to the standard output. We don't need to rewrite the whole method printInfo of the superclass in the subclass, but we use the statement super.printInfo();. The keyword super in the subclass Programmer refers to its superclass Employee.

Example 2
Employee.java
```java
public class Employee
{
   protected String name;
   protected int age;
   protected double salary;

   public void printInfo()
   {
      System.out.println("Name:      " + name);
      System.out.println("Age:       " + age);
      System.out.println("Salary:  $ " + salary);
   }
}
```

Programmer.java
```java
public class Programmer extends Employee
{
   String language;

   public void printInfo()
   {
      super.printInfo();
      System.out.println("Language:   " + language);
   }
}
```

TestEmployee.java
```java
public class TestEmployee
{
  public static void main(String[] args)
  {
    Employee emp = new Employee();
    Programmer prog = new Programmer();
    emp.name = "Jack";
    emp.age = 23;
    emp.salary = 2100.55;
    prog.name = "Emma";
    prog.age = 32;
    prog.salary = 3200.45;
    prog.language = "Java";
    emp.printInfo();
    prog.printInfo();
  }
}
```

If the code is executed the following is written to the standard output.

Name:	Jack
Age:	23
Salary:	$ 2100.55
Name:	Emma
Age:	32
Salary:	$ 3200.45
Language:	Java

12.1 Superclass constructor

When you instantiate an object of the subclass Programmer, the no-argument constructor of the superclass Employee is called. The following program writes **Peter Eva** to the standard output. By creating objects of the subclass Programmer, the no-argument constructor of the superclass Employee is called, and this one writes Peter to the standard output. Then the constructor of the subclass is called, and this one writes Eva to the standard output.

Example 3
Employee.java
```java
public class Employee
{
  protected String name;
  protected int age;
  protected double salary;

  public Employee()
```

```
  {
    System.out.print("Peter ");
  }
}
```

Programmer.java

```
public class Programmer extends Employee
{
  String language;

  public Programmer()
  {
    System.out.print("Eva");
  }
}
```

TestEmployee.java

```
public class TestEmployee
{
  public static void main(String[] args)
  {
    Programmer prog = new Programmer();
  }
}
```

If you pass the argument name to the constructor of the class Employee, the code will have an issue. The reason is that by creating the object prog, the no-argument constructor of the superclass is called.
If it does not exist, you need to call the constructor of the superclass explicitly. You can use the keyword super to call the constructor of the superclass.

Example 4

Employee.java

```
public class Employee
{
  protected String name;
  protected int age;
  protected double salary;

  public Employee(String name)
  {
    this.name = name;
    System.out.print(name + " ");
  }
}
```

Programmer.java

```java
public class Programmer extends Employee
{
  String language;

  public Programmer()
  {
    // Calling one-argument constructor of the superclass
    super("Peter");
    System.out.print("Eva");
  }
}
```

TestEmployee.java

```java
public class TestEmployee
{
  public static void main(String[] args)
  {
    Programmer prog = new Programmer();
  }
}
```

12.2. Overriding Methods

Overriding methods of super classes in subclasses allows the subclass to inherit and modify the behavior of the superclass as needed. The overridden method has the same name, type, and a number of parameters, and returns the same type of the data as the method that overrides.

See the method printInfo() in the example 2. Remember that you don't need to rewrite the printInfo() method of the super class Employee in the class Programmer. The keyword **super** allows you to access variables and methods of the superclass from the subclass.

The method printInfo in the superclass Employee.

```java
public void printInfo()
{
  System.out.println("Name:        " + name);
  System.out.println("Age:         " + age);
  System.out.println("Salary:    $ " + salary);
}
```

The subclass Programmer override the method printInfo of its superclass.

```java
public void printInfo()
{
  super.printInfo();
  System.out.println("Language:    " + language);
```

```
}
```

It is not necessary to rewrite the whole method printInfo of the superclass in the subclass. You can instead use the statement super.printInfo(); to access the method printInfo of the superclass.

12.3 Overloading Methods

Overloading of methods is the possibility to reuse the same method name in a class as often as needed. To do so the methods should comply with the following requirements:

The methods can have the same name and a different number of parameters, such as the method getNetSalary.

double getNetSalary()
double getNetSalary(**double** grossSalary)
double getNetSalary(**double** grossSalary, **int** taxRate)

The methods can have the same number of parameters, but their parameters may not have the same data types. Below is the method name getNetSalary reused and that is correct, because the data types of the parameters are different.

double getNetSalary(**double** grossSalary)
double getNetSalary(**int** taxRate)

The parameters of the methods can have the same number of parameters and the same data types, provided that the order of the parameters variable type is different.

double getNetSalary(**double** grossSalary, **int** taxRate)
double getNetSalary(**int** taxRate, **double** grossSalary)

Note: the following two methods do not have the requirements of the overloaded methods, although they return different data types.

int getNetSalary(**double** grossSalary)
double getNetSalary(**double** grossSalary)

See the method getNetSalary in the following program.

Example 5
```java
public class Employee
{
  public double getNetSalary()
  {
    double netSalary = 3000 - (3000 * 30) / 100;
    return netSalary;
  }
  public double getNetSalary(double grossSalary)
```

```
   {
      double netSalary = -(grossSalary * 30) / 100;
      return netSalary;
   }
   public double getNetSalary(int taxRate)
   {
      double netSalary = 2400 - (2400 * taxRate) / 100;
      return netSalary;
   }
   public double getNetSalary(double grossSalary, int taxRate)
   {
      double netSalary = grossSalary - (grossSalary * taxRate) / 100;
      return netSalary;
   }
   public double getNetSalary(int taxRate, double grossSalary)
   {
      double netSalary = grossSalary - (grossSalary * taxRate) / 100;
      return netSalary;
   }
   public static void main(String[] args)
   {
      Employee emp = new Employee();
      System.out.println(emp.getNetSalary());
      System.out.println(emp.getNetSalary(2500.65));
      System.out.println(emp.getNetSalary(25));
      System.out.println(emp.getNetSalary(2000.0, 35));
      System.out.println(emp.getNetSalary(40, 2000.0));
   }
}
```

The previous program writes the following to the standard output.

2100.0
-750.195
1800.0
1300.0
1200.0

Quiz 1: A simple inheritance example

What happens when the following program is compiled and run?

MySuper.java
```
public class MySuper
{
```

```
   protected int x;
}
```

MySub.java
```
public class MySub extends MySuper
{
   private int y = 3;

   MySub()
   {
      x += 2;
      y++;
      System.out.print(x + ", " + y);
   }
   public static void main(String[] args)
   {
      MySub ms = new MySub();
   }
}
```

Select the correct answer:
a. This code writes "0, 3" to the standard output.
b. This code writes "2, 3" to the standard output.
c. This code writes "2, 2" to the standard output.
d. This code writes "2, 4" to the standard output.
e. This code writes nothing to the standard output.
f. This code doesn't compile.

Explanation
The statement MySub ms = new MySub(); calls the no-argument constructor MySub().
The statement x += 2; adds 2 to the value of x of MySuper class.
The variable x is equal to 0, because it is not initialized.
x = 0 + 2 = 2.
the statement y++ adds one to the value of y.
y = 3 + 1 = 4

The correct answer is d.

Exercises
What is written to the standard output if the value of x = 5 and y = 8;
Compile and run the program to test your expectation.

Quiz 2: A superclass constructor

What happens when the following program is compiled and run?

MySuper.java

```java
public class MySuper
{
  protected int x = 1;

  MySuper()
  {
    x += 2;
  }
}
```

MySub.java

```java
public class MySub extends MySuper
{
  MySub(int y)
  {
    x += y;
  }
  public static void main(String[] args)
  {
    MySub ms = new MySub(4);
    System.out.print(ms.x);
  }
}
```

Select the correct answer:

a. This code writes "7" to the standard output.

b. This code writes "5" to the standard output.

c. This code writes "1" to the standard output.

d. This code writes "0" to the standard output.

e. This code writes nothing to the standard output.

f. This code doesn't compile.

Explanation

The statement MySub ms = new MySub(3); instantiate the object ms.

It calls the no-argument constructor of the super class, which adds 2 to the value of x.

x = 1 + 2 = 3;

By creating the object ms, the program calls the one-argument constructor of MySub.

the parameter y = 4.

x += y; is equivalent to x = 3 + 4 = 7;

The correct answer is a.

Exercises

Create a new MySub object called ms2, and pass the value 6 to the constructor.

What would be the x value of the ms2 object?

Quiz 3: Overriding methods

What happens when the following program is compiled and run?

MySuper.java
```java
public class MySuper
{
  protected char c = 'G';

  void method()
  {
    System.out.print(c);
  }
}
```

MySub.java
```java
class MySub extends MySuper
{
  char c2 = 'A';

  MySub()
  {
    this('N');
    System.out.print(c2);
  }
  MySub(char c)
  {
    System.out.print(c);
  }
  @Override
  void method()
  {
    super.method();
    System.out.print(c2);
  }
  public static void main(String[] args)
  {
    MySub mySub = new MySub();
    mySub.method();
  }
}
```

Select the correct answer:

a. This code writes "NGA" to the standard output.

b. This code writes "NAGA" to the standard output.

c. This code writes "AGA" to the standard output.

d. This code writes "GA" to the standard output.

e. This code writes nothing to the standard output.

f. This code doesn't compile.

Explanation

The statement MySub mySub = new MySub(); calls the the no-argument constructor of MySub class.

The statement this('N'); calls the one-argument constructor of MySub class, which prints "N" to the standard output.

The statement System.out.print(c2); prints "A" to the standard output.

The statement mySub.method(); invokes the method.

The statement super.method(); calls the method in the super class which prints "G" to the standard output.

The statement System.out.print(c2); prints "A" to the standard output.

The result is NAGA

The correct answer is b.

Exercises

What would be the result if you add the following constructor to MySuper class? MySuper() {
    System.out.print('Q');
}

Test your program to test your expectation.

Quiz 4: A complicated inheritance

What happens when the following program is compiled and run?

SuperB.java
```java
public class SuperB
{
  protected int x = 3;

  public SuperB()
  {
    x += 2;
    System.out.print(" x" + x);
  }
}
```

SuperA.java
```java
public class SuperA extends SuperB
{
```

```
   int y = 7;

   public SuperA()
   {
      y++;
      System.out.print(" y" + y);
   }
}
```

MySub.java
```
public class MySub extends SuperA
{
   public MySub()
   {
      x += 2;
      y += 3;
      System.out.print(" x" + x);
      System.out.print(" y" + y);
   }
   public static void main(String[] args)
   {
      MySub mySub = new MySub();
   }
}
```

Select the correct answer:

a. This code writes "x5 y10" to the standard output.

b. This code writes "y8 x5 y11" to the standard output.

c. This code writes "x5 y8 x7 y11" to the standard output.

d. This code writes "x0 y0" to the standard output.

e. This code writes nothing to the standard output.

f. This code doesn't compile.

Explanation

The statement MySub mySub = new MySub(); calls the no-argument constructor of the superclass SuperA. The SuperA constructor calls the no-argument constructor of the SuperB, which adds 2 to the value of x.
x = 2 + 3 = 5.
The statement System.out.print(" x" + x); prints x5 to the standard output.

The SuperA constructor increments the value of y by one.
y = 7 + 1 = 8.
The statement System.out.print(" y" + y); prints y8 to the standard output.

The constructor MySub() adds 2 to the value of x.
The last value of x of the class SuperA is 5.
x = 5 + 2 = 7.

The statement y += 3 increments the value of y by 3.

y = 8 + 3 = 11;

The statement System.out.print(" y" + y); prints y11 to the standard output.

The correct answer is c.

Exercises

Add an integer variable called x (not initialized) to the class MySub.

What would be the result if you compile and run the program?

Quiz 5: Overriding methods

What happens when the following program is compiled and run?

MySuper.java
```java
public class MySuper
{
  protected int x = 2;

  int method(int i)
  {
    return x + i;
  }
}
```

MySub.java
```java
public class MySub extends MySuper
{
  int method(int i, int i2)
  {
    return method(i) + x + i2;
  }
  public static void main(String[] args)
  {
    MySub mySub = new MySub();
    System.out.print(mySub.method(3, 6));
  }
}
```

Select the correct answer:

a. This code writes "12" to the standard output.

b. This code writes "13" to the standard output.

c. This code writes "11" to the standard output.

d. This code writes "14" to the standard output.

e. This code writes nothing to the standard output.

f. This code doesn't compile.

Explanation

The statement MySub mySub = new MySub(); calls the no-argument constructor of the MySub class. The statement System.out.print(mySub.method(3,6)); invokes the one parameter method of the the class MySuper. It returns $x + i = 2 + 3 = 5$;

method(i) + x + i2 = $5 + 2 + 6 = 13$.

The correct answer is b.

Exercises

Replace the values of the parameters of the statement "System.out.print(mySub.method(3,6));" with (2,8). What would be printed to the standard output?

Quiz 6: Using the keyword super

What happens when the following program is compiled and run?

MySuper.java
```java
public class MySuper
{
  protected int x = 3;
  protected char e = 'd';

  void myMethod()
  {
    x += 4;
    System.out.print(e);
    System.out.print(x);
  }
}
```

MySub.java
```java
public class MySub extends MySuper
{
  void myMethod()
  {
    x++;
    System.out.print(e);
    super.myMethod();
    x += 2;
    System.out.print(x);
  }
  public static void main(String[] args)
  {
```

```
      MySub ms = new MySub();
      ms.myMethod();
   }
}
```

Select the correct answer:
a. This code writes "dd79" to the standard output.
b. This code writes "dd89" to the standard output.
c. This code writes "d6" to the standard output.
d. This code writes "dd810" to the standard output.
e. This code doesn't compile.

Explanation
The statement ms.myMethod(), invokes the overridden method myMethod of the subclass.
x++ increments the value of x by 1.
x = 3 + 1 = 4.
System.out.print(e), prints the letter "d" to the standard output.

The statement super.mythod(), invokes the method myMethod of the superclass.
x+=4 increments the value of x by 4.
x = 4 + 4 = 8.
System.out.print(e), prints the letter "d" to the standard output.
System.out.print(x), prints "8" to the standard output, because that is the current value of x.

Back to the overridden method myMethod of the subclass.
x+= 2, adds 2 to the value of x.
x = 8 + 2 = 10.
The statement System.out.print(x), prints the current value of x, which is 10.

The correct answer is d.

Exercises
Declare a char variable called "e". Assign the value "p" to it.
What is written to the standard output if you execute the code?

Quiz 7: Using the keywords super and this to call constructors

What happens when the following program is compiled and run?

MySuper.java
```
public class MySuper
{
   MySuper(String name)
   {
      this(name, "d");
      System.out.print(name);
```

```
  }
  MySuper(String name, String name2)
  {
    System.out.print(name);
    System.out.print(name2);
  }
}
```

MySub.java
```
public class MySub extends MySuper
{
  MySub(String name)
  {
    super(name);
    System.out.print(name);
  }
  public static void main(String[] args)
  {
    MySub ms = new MySub("x");
  }
}
```

Select the correct answer:

a. This code writes "xdd" to the standard output.

b. This code writes "xd" to the standard output.

c. This code writes "dxx" to the standard output.

d. This code writes "xdxx" to the standard output.

e. This code writes "xx" to the standard output.

f. This code doesn't compile.

Explanation

The statement MySub ms = new MySub("x"), calls the one-argument constructor of mySub.

The statement super(name), calls the one-argument constructor of MySuper class and passes the arguments "x" to it.

The statement this(name, "d"), calls the two-argument constructor of MySuper class, and passes the arguments "x" and "d" to it.

The statement System.out.print(name), prints x to the standard output.

The statement System.out.print(name2), prints "d" to the standard output.

The statement System.out.print(name); prints another x to the standard output.

Back to the MySub one-argument constructor.

The statement System.out.print(name), prints "x" to the standard output.

The correct answer is d.

Exercises

Replace the String parameter "name" at the statement super(name); with "s" in the class MySub
What is written to the standard output if the program is executed?

Quiz 8: Inheritance from different packages

What happens when the following program is compiled and run?
MySuper.java

```java
package package_02;

public class MySuper
{
  public String str1 = "String 1";
  protected String str2 = "String 2";
  String str3 = "String 3";
  private String str4 = "String 4";
}
```

MySub.java

```java
package package_01;

import package_02.MySuper;

public class MySub extends MySuper
{
  public static void main(String[] args)
  {
    MySuper mySuper = new MySuper();
    MySub mySub = new MySub();
    // System.out.print(mySuper.str1); /* 1 */
    // System.out.print(mySuper.str2); /* 2 */
    // System.out.print(mySuper.str3); /* 3 */
    // System.out.print(mySuper.str4); /* 4 */
    // System.out.print(mySub.str2); /* 5 */
  }
}
```

Which statement(s) are true? Choose all that apply.

a. If statement 1 is uncommented, the code writes "String 1" to the standard output.
b. If statement 2 is uncommented, the code writes "String 2" to the standard output.
c. If statement 3 is uncommented, the code writes "String 3" to the standard output.
d. If statement 4 is uncommented, the code writes "String 4" to the standard output.
e. If statement 5 is uncommented, the code writes "String 2" to the standard output.

Explanation

a. The subclass MySub has access to all the public members of the class MySuper.

b, c, d are incorrect, because the two classes are in different packages and their access modifiers restrict the access from outside the package. Remember that mySub object has no access to to even protected members of MySuper objects.

e. The objects of MySub can access all the protected members of its superclass MySuper.

The correct answers are a, e.

Exercises

Declare a protected integer variable called myInt in the class MySuper.

Which one of the two objects mySuper and mySub can access myInt variable?

Add apiece of code to the class MySub, compile and run the program to test your expectation.

Assignment: Inheritance and overriding methods

Create three new classes namely Car , Truck and Vehicle.

We want to know about cars the brand, manufacture year, color and maximum number of passengers that fits in it.

We want to know about trucks the brand, manufacture year, color and the maximum allowable load.

Create two car objects and two truck objects, see the information below.

Create another class with a main method to test the program.

Write a method to print all the information about the cars and the trucks to the standard output. Use inheritance to make your code reusable. If your program is compiled and run, the following is written to the standard output.

```
----------------Car-----------------------
Brand:               Toyota
Manufacture year:        2013
Color:               red
Max passengers: 5
----------------Car-----------------------
Brand:               Mazda
Manufacture year:        2017
Color:               blue
Max passengers: 8
----------------Truck--------------
Brand:               BMW
Manufacture year:        2016
Color:               green
Maximum Load:            6550.0
----------------Truck--------------
Brand:               Volvo
Manufacture year:        2014
Color:               black
Maximum Load:            4000.0
```

13. Final Classes & the Final Keyword

13.1. What Is A Final Class?

Declaring a class final prevents programmers to use it as a superclass.
A final class in Java is a class that cannot be extended or cannot be subclassed, but it can be a subclass of another class.

13.2. What Is A Final Method?

A final method is a method that cannot be overridden in sub classes.
By declaring the method getSum final, you guarantee that the method cannot be overridden in subclasses of MyClass.

Example 1
```java
public class MyClass
{
  final int getSum(int x, int y)
  {
    return x + y;
  }
}
```

13.3. What Is A Final Variable?

A final variable is actually a constant and its value may not be changed once it is initialized. In the following example, the method changeIP tries to change the value of the final variable PI, but that causes an error in the program. The reason is that a final variable is a constant.

Example 2
```java
public class Circle
{
  final double PI = 3.14;

  void changePI()
  {
    PI++;
  }
}
```

Quiz 1: Final variables

What happens when the following program is compiled and run?

```java
public class MyClass
{
  final int x = 3;

  int getResult(int y, int z)
  {
    if (y >= z)
    {
      return y + x;
    }
    else
    {
      // y = 5; /* 1 */
      // z += 3; /* 2 */
      // z = x / 2; /* 3 */
      // int x = 6; /* 4 */
      // x ++; /* 5 */
      return z + x;
    }
  }
  public static void main(String[] args)
  {
    MyClass mc = new MyClass();
    System.out.println(mc.getResult(4, 6));
  }
}
```

Choose all the correct statements.
a. If comment 1 is turned off, this code cannot be compiled.
b. If comment 2 is turned off, this code cannot be compiled.
c. If comment 3 is turned off, this code cannot be compiled.
d. If comment 4 is turned off, this code cannot be compiled.
e. If comment 5 is turned off, this code cannot be compiled.

Explanation
By turning off the comments a, b, c and d, the code can be compiled.
The fifth statement x ++; tries to change the value of the variable x, but that is not allowed. The reason is that the variable x is final and that makes him a constant.
The only correct answer is e.

Exercises

If you add the keyword final to the class MyClass:

Is it possible for MyClass to extend another class?

Is it possible for other classes to extend MyClass?

Quiz 2: Final methods

Which of the following statements causes an error if you try to replace the name of the method myMethod?

MySuper.java
```java
public class MySuper
{
    final void methodA()
    {
        System.out.print("x");
    }
    final void methodB(int i)
    {
        System.out.print("x" + i);
    }
    final void methodC(String str)
    {
        System.out.print("x");
    }
}
```

MyClass.java
```java
public class MyClass extends MySuper
{
    int z = 5;

    void myMethod(int x)
    {
        System.out.print("x");
    }
    public static void main(String[] args)
    {
        MyClass mc = new MyClass();
    }
}
```

Select the correct answer:

a. The names methodA, methodB and methodC are not allowed.

b. The names methodB and methodC are not allowed .

c. The name methodB is not allowed.

d. The name methodC is not allowed.

Explanation

It is not allowed to override final methods.

Since the superclass MySuper contains a final method methodB(int i) with one int-argument, this method matches the method with one int-argument in the subclass.

That is the reason that only the name methodB is not allowed.

The other method names, with no-argument or different type of arguments, are allowed.

The correct answer is c.

Question

Can you add the following method to the class MyClass without causing errors in the program?

int methodB(**int** x)
{
  System.*out*.print("x");
  return x;
}

Quiz 3: Final methods and variables

What happens when the following program is compiled and run?

MySuper.java
```
public class MySuper
{
   final int x = 4;

   final String methodA(int i, String s)
   {
      String str = i + ", " + s;
      return str;
   }
}
```

MyClass.java
```java
public class MyClass extends MySuper
{
   int x = 3;

   String methodA(String s, int i)
   {
      String str = s + ", " + i;
      return str;
   }
   public static void main(String[] args)
   {
      MySuper ms = new MySuper();
      System.out.print(ms.methodA(23, "Emma"));
   }
}
```

Select the correct answer:

a. This program writes Emma, 23" to the standard output.

b. This program writes 23, Emma" to the standard output.

c. This program has a problem, because methodA is final and it is overridden in the subclass.

d. This program has a problem, because the variable int x is final in the superclass and you can't use it in the subclass.

Explanation

claim c is incorrect because the methodA has different arguments in the subclass, which cannot be considered as overriding methods.

claim d is incorrect, because int x is another variable and it is not considered as changing value of the final variable in the superclass.

The statement System.out.print(ms.methodA(23,"Emma")); invokes methodA of the superclass, and that is why the age is printed before the name Emma.

The correct answer is: b

Exercises

Does this program work if we add the statement super.x++; right under the statement String str = s + ", " + i; in the methodA of the class MyClass

Clarify your answer.

Quiz 4: Final methods and variables

What happens when the following program is compiled and run?

MySuper.java
```java
public class MySuper
{
   final void methodA(int x, double y)
   {
      double z = x * y;
      System.out.print(z);
   }
}
```

MyClass.java
```java
public final class MyClass extends MySuper
{
   void methodA(int x, int y)
   {
      int z = x - y;
      System.out.print(z);
   }
   public static void main(String[] args)
   {
      MyClass mc = new MyClass();
      mc.methodA(5, 3.0);
   }
}
```

Select the correct answer:

a. This program writes "2.0" to the standard output.

b. This program writes "15.0" to the standard output.

c. This program writes "15" to the standard output.

d. This program has a problem, because methodA is final, but it seems to be overridden in the class MyClass.

e. This program has a problem, because MyClass is final and it extends another class.

Explanation

claim d is incorrect, because the methodA has different types of arguments.

claim e is incorrect, because final classes are allowed to extend other classes.

The statement mc.methodA(5, 3.0) matches the methodA of the subclass.

The statement mc.methodA(5, 3.0); applies to the method in the superclass, because it has the same types of parameters.

The double variable $z = z = x * y = 5 * 3.0 = 15.0$

The correct answer is b.

Exercises

What is written to the standard output if you replace the statement mc.methodA(5,3.0); with the statement mc.methodA(6,4)?

Compile and run the program to check out your expectation.

Assignment: How to use the class Math in the Java standard-API

Create a class MyCalculation. You don't need to import the class Math in your class because it is in the package java.long. This package is automatically imported in all your classes.

Try to extend the class Math in your class.

What would be your explanation if you cannot use the class Math as superclass for your class?

Do you need to create objects of the class Math to use its methods?

Which method of the class Math provides the larger number of two numbers? Use that method, and pass the numbers 35 and 46 as parameter by the method to check the result.

Find the smaller number of the numbers 46.98 and 44.99.

Find the square root of the number 81.0.

14. Abstract Classes

14.1. What is an abstract class?

An abstract class is a class in which one or more methods are abstract. All abstract classes and abstract methods are provided with the keyword abstract. An abstract method has no body and it is not defined, but only declared. In the following example, the method getArea is abstract, therefore it has no body.

protected abstract double getArea();

It is important to know that you cannot instantiate objects from abstract classes, because they are incomplete. A subclass of an abstract class must override all its abstract methods, otherwise, it cannot be instantiated either.

14.2. Important concepts of abstract classes and methods

You cannot instantiate abstract classes.
The main purpose of abstract classes is extending them and overriding their methods.
When a class contains one or more abstract methods, It should be declared abstract.
Abstract methods do not have a body.
A class can be declared abstract even if they do not contain abstract methods.

14.3. Subclasses of abstract classes

A subclass of an abstract class must override all the abstract methods of its superclass, otherwise, it should also be declared abstract.
It is possible to instantiate a subclass of an abstract class that overrides all the abstract methods of its superclass.
A subclass of an abstract class can also be declared abstract.

14.4. Using abstract classes

An example of using abstract classes is the two-dimensional shape. All 2D shapes have an area and a circumference. By creating a class shape and declaring the two abstract methods getArea and getPerimeter, we enforce any class that extends the class shape implement those two methods. If a subclass does not override these two methods, it should also be declared abstract. In the following example, we enforce the subclasses Rectangle and Circle to override the methods getArea and getPerimeter of their superclass Shape.

Don't forget that subclasses of the class Shape can override the abstract methods on their own way, as shown in the following example.

Example
Shape.java
```java
public abstract class Shape
{
  protected abstract double getArea();
  protected abstract double getPerimeter();
}
```

Rectangle.java

```java
public class Rectangle extends Shape
{
  private double width;
  private double length;

  public Rectangle(double width, double length)
  {
    this.width = width;
    this.length = length;
  }
  public double getArea()
  {
    return width * length;
  }
  public double getPerimeter()
  {
    return 2 * (width + length);
  }
}
```

Circle.java

```java
public class Circle extends Shape
{
  private double radius;
  final double PI = 3.14;

  public Circle(double radius)
  {
    this.radius = radius;
  }
  public double getArea()
  {
    return PI * radius * radius;
  }
  public double getPerimeter()
  {
    return 2 * PI * radius;
  }
}
```

Test.java

```java
public class Test
{
  public static void main(String[] args)
  {
    Rectangle rec = new Rectangle(6, 8);
    Circle cir = new Circle(4.0);

    System.out.println("Rectangle area:      " + rec.getArea());
    System.out.println("Rectangle perimeter: " + rec.getPerimeter());
    System.out.println("Circle area:         " + cir.getArea());
    System.out.println("Circle perimeter:    " + cir.getPerimeter());
  }
}
```

If this code is executed, the following is written to the standard output.

Rectangle area: 48.0

Rectangle perimeter: 28.0

Circle area: 50.24

Circle perimeter: 25.12

Quiz 1: Extending an abstract class

What happens when the following program is compiled and run?

MyAbstract.java

```java
public abstract class MyAbstract
{
  protected int x = 6;

  public MyAbstract()
  {
    x += 2;
  }
  abstract int getSum(int x);
}
```

MyClass.java

```java
public class MyClass extends MyAbstract
{
  int getSum()
  {
    return x + 5;
  }
  int getSum(int x)
```

```
  {
    return super.x + x;
  }
  public static void main(String[] args)
  {
    MyClass mc = new MyClass();
    System.out.print(mc.getSum(4));
  }
}
```

Which claim(s) are true? (Choose all that apply.)

Select all the correct answers.

a. It is not allowed to change the name of the method getSum() (no-arg) of the class MyClass.

b. It is not allowed to change the name of the method getSum(int x) of the class MyClass.

c. By executing this code, 12 is printed to the standard output.

d. By executing this code, 10 is printed to the standard output.

Explanation

You can change the method name getSum() no-argument to any name you wish, but the getSum(int x) one-argument overrides the method in the abstract super class.

Any class that extends an abstract class must override all its abstract methods, otherwise, you cannot instantiate it.

The initial value of x is equal to 6.

The statement MyClass mc = new MyClass(); creates an object of the type of MyClass, which calls the no-argument constructor of the superclass MyAbstract class.

The statement x += 2; adds 2 to the value of x.

x = 6 + 2 = 8;

The statement System.out.print(mc.getSum(4)); invokes the method getSum(int arg) and prints the result to the standard output.

super.x + x = 8 + 4 = 12.

The correct answers are b and c.

Exercises

Add an abstract method printName that does not return value with one string parameter.

abstract void printMyName(String name);

Override the method printName in the class MyClass. The method should write the value of the parameter name to the standard output.

Compile and run the program to test the code.

Quiz 2: A subclass of a subclass of an abstract class

What happens when the following program is compiled and run?

MyAbstract.java

```java
public abstract class MyAbstract
{
  MyAbstract()
  {
    System.out.print("n");
  }
  abstract void printLetter(char c);
}
```

MySuper.java

```java
public class MySuper extends MyAbstract
{
  MySuper()
  {
  }
  MySuper(int i)
  {
    System.out.print(i);
  }
  void printLetter(char c)
  {
    System.out.print(c);
  }
}
```

MySub.java

```java
public class MySub extends MySuper
{
  MySub()
  {
    System.out.print("p");
  }
  public static void main(String[] args)
  {
    new MySub().printLetter('s');
  }
}
```

Select the correct answer:

a. This code writes ps to the standard output.

b. This code writes pns to the standard output.

c. This code writes spn to the standard output.

d. This code requires nsip to the standard output.

e. This code requires nps to the standard output.

f. This code writes nothing to the standard output.

Explanation

The statement

new MySub().printLetter('s'); creates a new object of the subclass.

By creating a new object of the Subclass the no-argument constructor of its superclass is called and this calls the no-argument constructor of its superclass MyAbstract.

The statement System.out.print("n"); writes n to the standard output.

The no-argument constructor of the Superclass writes nothing to the standard output.

The no-argument constructor of the Subclass writes p to the standard output.

The statement MySub.printLetter('s'); invokes the method printLetter.

This writes the parameter s of the method to the standard output.

The correct answer is e.

Exercises

What is written to the standard output if you add the statement super(10); right above the statement System.out.print("p"); in the class MySub?

Compile and run the program to check.

Quiz 3: Demonstrating an abstract class

What happens when the following program is compiled and run?

MyAbstract.java
```
abstract class MyAbstract
{
  String str = "N";

  MyAbstract()
  {
    this("O");
    str += "L";
  }
  MyAbstract(String str)
  {
    str += str;
  }
}
```

MyClass.java
```java
public class MyClass extends MyAbstract
{
    MyClass()
    {
        this(2);
        str += 7;
    }
    MyClass(int x)
    {
        str += x;
    }
    public static void main(String[] args)
    {
        MyClass mc = new MyClass();
        System.out.print(mc.str);
    }
}
```

Select the correct answer:
a. This code writes "NL27" to the standard output.
b. This code writes "NOL27" to the standard output.
c. This code writes "N27" to the standard output.
d. This code writes "27NL" to the standard output.
e. This code writes "27NOL" to the standard output.
f. This code does not compile.

Explanation
By instantiating the object mc, the no-argument constructor of the superclass is invoked.
string str = "N";
The statement this("O"); adds nothing to the value of str, because the one-argument constructor MyAbstract(String str) {str += str;} refers to the parameter str not the instance variable.
The statement str += "L"; adds "L" to the value of the str.
The value of str becomes "NL".
The no-argument constructor of the class MyClass calls the one-argument constructor, which adds 2 to the value of the str.
At last the statment str += 7; adds also 7 to the value of the String.

The correct answer is a.

Exercises
What is written to the standard output if you replace the statemen str += str; in the class MyAbstract with the statement this.str += str;?

Execute the program to test the result.

Quiz 4: A constructor chain

What happens when the following program is compiled and run?

MyClassB.java
```java
public abstract class MyClassB
{
  MyClassB()
  {
    System.out.print("a");
  }
}
```

MyClassA.java
```java
public class MyClassA extends MyClassB
{
  MyClassA()
  {
    System.out.print("b");
  }
  MyClassA(int i)
  {
    System.out.print("d" + i);
  }
}
```

MyClass.java
```java
public class MyClass extends MyClassA
{
  MyClass(int i)
  {
    System.out.print("c" + i);
  }
  public static void main(String[] args)
  {
    new MyClass(4);
    new MyClassA(4);
  }
}
```

Select the correct answer:
a. This code writes "c4d4" to the standard output.
b. This code writes "abc4d4" to the standard output.

c. This code writes "c4" to the standard output.

d. This code writes "c4bd4" to the standard output.

e. This code writes "abc4ad4" to the standard output.

f. This code does not compile.

Explanation

By instantiating MyClass, the no-argument constructor of the superclass MyClassA is called.

By calling the constructor of MyClassA, the program calls the no-argument constructor of the superclass MyClassB.

The no-argument constructor of MyClassB, prints "a" to the standard output.

The no-argument constructor of MyClassA, prints "b" to the standard output.

The one-argument constructor of MyClass System.out.print("c" + i), prints "c4" to the standard output. That is because the parameter i = 4.

The statement MyClassA(i) which has the parameter 4. It calls the no-argument constructor of MyClassB(), which prints "a" to the standard output.

By passing 4 to the one-argument constructor of MyClassA, "d4" is printed to the standard output.

The correct answer is e.

Exercises

Add the abstract method public abstract int getResult(int x, int y); to the class MyClassB.

Fix the error that caused by step 1 if you know that the method getResult(int x, int y) should find the result of (x * y)

Quiz 5: Overriding abstract methods

What happens when the following program is compiled and run?

MyAbstract.java
```
public abstract class MyAbstract
{
   int x;

   abstract void methodA();
   abstract String methodB(String s);
}
```

MyClass.java
```
public class MyClass extends MyAbstract
{
   void methodA()
   {
     System.out.print("x");
```

```java
  }
  void methodA(int x)
  {
    System.out.print("y" + x);
  }
  String methodB(String s)
  {
    return s + x;
  }
  String methodB(int x)
  {
    return "x" + x;
  }
  public static void main(String[] args)
  {
    MyClass mc = new MyClass();
    mc.methodA();
    System.out.print(mc.methodB("y"));
  }
}
```

Which claim(s) are true? (Choose all that apply.)

Select all the correct answers.

a. Removing the method void methodA() from the class MyClass, causes error.

b. Removing the method void methodA(int x) from the class MyClass, causes error.

c. Removing the method String methodB(String s) from the class MyClass, causes error.

d. Removing the method String methodB(int x) from the class MyClass, causes error.

e. By executing this code, xy0 is written to the standard output.

f. By executing this code, xy is written to the standard output.

Only removing the methods (void methodA() and the method String methodB(String s)) cause errors, because they override the abstract methods of the class MyAbstract. By removing those two methods from the class MyClass, you need to declare MyClass also abstract.

The statement MyClass mc = new MyClass(), creates the object mc.

The statement mc.methodA(), invokes the methodA(), which prints "x" to the standard output.

The statement System.out.print(mc.methodB("y")), invokes the methodB(String s), which returns s + x. s is the parameter "y" and x is the value of x.

The value of x is by default 0, because it is not initialized.

The correct answers are a, c and e.

Exercises

The following method is not abstract. Can you add it to the class MyAbstract?

public double getPrice(**double** price)
{
    return price;
}

Abstract classes cannot be instantiated. If adding the previous method is possible, how can you invoke it?
Add a piece of code to invoke the method getPrice if the previous steps are possible.

Assignment: What is the current date and time?

Search the Calendar class in the Java standard API. You can find the link to the API in the beginning of this book.

Read the description of the method getInstance() from the class Calendar.
Find the method getTime() of the class Calendar.
Use the Calendar class and its methods to write the current date and time to the standard output.

If your answer is correct, your program writes the current date and time to the standard output, as follows:
Fri Jun 30 10:46:27 CEST 2017

15. Interfaces

Java allows to inherit from only a single class, but it supports multiple inheritance from interfaces. Implementing interfaces, offers a solution for objects that have multiple characteristics. To implement an interface the keyword implements is used. The name of the interface starts as a class name with a capital letter.

15.1. What Are Interfaces And Why They Are Used?

Subclasses that inherit a single superclass are related, but unrelated classes can implement the same interface.
Interfaces offer the advantage of multiple inheritance in Java.
Interfaces do not have constructors and cannot be instantiated.
Interfaces are implemented by classes using the keyword implements, but they are extended by other interfaces using the keyword extends.
If more than one interface is implemented, the names of the interfaces are separated by a comma.

15.2. Interface Methods

All the methods in an interface are implicitly abstract.
A class that implements an interface must override all the methods of that interface.
Interface methods that are overridden by a class should be declared public.

15.3. Interface Constants

By default constants of an interface are public, static and final even if no modifiers is mentioned.
Interface constants must be initialized.
It is not allowed to declare interface constants private or protected.

15.4. How to implement an interface?

In the following example the class MyArray implements the interface List

```
public class MyArray implements List { }
```

The List interface extends the interface List2.

```
public interface List extends List2 {}
```

The class MyArray extends the class MyArray2 and implements the interface
List.

```
public class MyArray extends MyArray2 implements List { }
```

The class MyArray extends the class MyArray2 and implements the two interfaces,
List and List2.

```
public class MyArray extends MyArray2 implements List,List2 { }
```

In the following example, the items Tablet and TV contains a method that calculates the prices with discount. To enforce this functionality, the item classes should implement the interface **ItemInterface**.

The interface ItemInterface contains an abstract method, namely getDiscountPrice. In our example, for tablets there is a discount for students, for TVs, there is a discount for people who are older than 60 years.

Example
ItemInterface.java
```java
public interface ItemInterface
{
   double getDiscountPrice();
}
```

Tablet.java
```java
public class Tablet implements ItemInterface
{
   double price = 350;
   double discount = 0.20;
   boolean isStudent;

   public double getDiscountPrice()
   {
     // extra discount for students
     if (isStudent)
     {
       discount = 0.25;
     }
     return price - (price * discount);
   }
}
```

TV.java
```java
public class TV implements ItemInterface
{
   double price = 420;
   double discount = 0.30;
   boolean isOlderThanSixty;

   public double getDiscountPrice()
   {
     // extra discount for older than sixty years
     if (isOlderThanSixty)
     {
       discount = 0.40;
     }
     return price - (price * discount);
   }
}
```

TestProgram
```java
public class TestProgram
{
  public static void main(String[] args)
  {
    TV tv = new TV();
    TV tv2 = new TV();
    tv.isOlderThanSixty = true;
    tv2.isOlderThanSixty = false;
    Tablet tab = new Tablet();
    Tablet tab2 = new Tablet();
    tab.isStudent = true;
    tab2.isStudent = false;
    System.out.println("TV");
    System.out.println("Extra discount: "+tv.getDiscountPrice());
    System.out.println("Normal discount: "+tv2.getDiscountPrice());
    System.out.println("Tablet");
    System.out.println("Extra discount: "+tab.getDiscountPrice());
    System.out.println("Normal discount: "+tab2.getDiscountPrice());
  }
}
```

This program writes the following to the standard output.

TV
Extra discount: 252.0
Normal discount: 294.0
Tablet
Extra discount: 262.5
Normal discount: 280.0

Quiz 1: Implementing an interface

What happens when the following program is compiled and run?

MyInterface.java
```java
public interface MyInterface
{
  int x = 5;

  void method();
  void method(int i);
}
```

MyClass.java
```java
public class MyClass implements MyInterface
{
  public void method()
  {
```

```
    // x++; /* 1*/
    System.out.print(x);
  }
  public void method(int i)
  {
    int z = i;
    // z = z + x; /* 2*/
    method();
    System.out.print(z);
  }
  public static void main(String[] args)
  {
    new MyClass().method(4);
  }
}
```

Which are true? Choose all the correct answers.

a. This code does not compile.

b. If this code is compiled and run, the output is 54.

c. If the statement 1 is uncommented, the output is 60.

d. If the statement 1 is uncommented, this code does not compile.

e. If the statement 2 is uncommented, the output is 59.

f. If the statement 2 is uncommented, this code does not compile.

Explanation

This code is fine and its output is 54.

Constants of an interface are by default public, static and final.

The Statement 1 tries to change the value of x and that causes error.

The statement 2 doesn't try to change the value of x, but it reassigns the z variable.

By un-commenting statement 2, the value of z becomes $z + i = 4 + 5 = 9$.

The statement System.out.print(z); prints the value of z to the standard output, which is 9.

The correct answers are b, d and e.

Exercises

What would be the result of exectuting this program if you add the following two statements directly above the statement new Myclass.method(4); ?

int x = 7;

x ++;

Quiz 2: Implementing two interfaces

What happens when the following program is compiled and run?

InterfaceA.java

```
public interface InterfaceA
{
  void myMethod();
  void myMethod(char c);
}
```

InterfaceB.java
```java
public interface InterfaceB
{
  int MAX_ALLOWED = 3;

  int getSum();
}
```

MyClass.java
```java
public class MyClass implements InterfaceA,InterfaceB
{
  // int MAX_ALLOWED; /*1*/
  int z = 2;

  public void myMethod()
  {
    z = MAX_ALLOWED + 4;
    System.out.print("H");
  }
  public void myMethod(char j)
  {
    // MAX_ALLOWED += 3; /* 2*/
    myMethod();
    System.out.print(j);
    System.out.print(z);
  }
  public int getSum()
  {
    return MAX_ALLOWED + z;
  }
  public static void main(String[] args)
  {
    MyClass mk = new MyClass();
    mk.myMethod('K');
  }
}
```

Which are true? Choose all the correct answers.

a. This code does not compile.

b. If this code is compiled and run, the output is "HK2".

c. If this code is compiled and run, the output is "HK7".

d. Removing the method som() from MyClass, doesn't cause errors.

e. If the statement 2 is uncommented, we can compile and run the code.

f. If both statements 1 and 2 are uncommented, we can compile and run the code.

Explanation

a. is false because the code is fine.

b. is false.

c. The statement mk.mijnMethode('K'), invokes the method mijnMethode with char argument.

The statement mijnMethode(), invokes the no-argument mijnMethode(), which changes the value of z.

z = x + 4;

z = 7.

The statement System.out.print("H"), prints "H" to the standard output.

The statement System.out.print(j), prints "K" to the standard output.

The statement System.out.print(z), prints the last value of z which is 7 to the standard output.

d. Removing the method som(), causes an error because MyClass implements both interfaces and it needs to override all their methods.

e. We cannot compile and run the code, because "MAX_TOEGESTAAN" refers to the MAX_TOEGESTAAN of the interfaceB and that is by default final.

It is not allowed to change the value of constants.

f. By removing both of the statement, the code will be fine. We can then change the value of MAX_TOEGESTAAN, because in that case, it refers to the variable MAX_TOEGESTAAN of MyClass not the one of the interfaceB.

The correct answers are c and f.

Exercises

What would be the result if you replace the statement "mc.myMethod('K');" in the main method with "mc.myMethod();"?

Compile and run the code to test the result.

Quiz 3: An abstract class implements an interfaces

What happens when the following program is compiled and run?

MyInterface.java
```java
public interface MyInterface
{
   int x = 4;

   void myMethod();
   void myMethod(String str);
}
```

MySuper.java
```java
public abstract class MySuper implements MyInterface
{
   public void myMethod()
   {
     System.out.print("m" + x);
   }
}
```

MyClass.java
```java
public class MyClass extends MySuper
{
  int x = 6;

  public void myMethod(String s)
  {
    myMethod();
    System.out.print("q" + s + x);
  }
  public static void main(String[] args)
  {
    MyClass mc = new MyClass();
    mc.myMethod("w");
  }
}
```

Which are true? Choose all the correct answers.

a. MySuper must implement all the methods of MyInterface.

b. This code does not compile, because MySuper is abstract.

c. If this code is compiled and run, the output is "m4qw6".

d. If this code is compiled and run, the output is "m6qw6".

e. If this code is compiled and run, the output is "m4qw4".

Explanation

a. MySuper is declared abstract, and that is why it is not necessary to implement all the methods of MyInterface.

b. False.

c. The statement mk.mijnMethode("w"); invokes the one-argument mijnMethode, which invokes the no-argument mijnMethode of MySuper class.

The statement System.out.print("m" + x); prints m4 to the standard output, because MySuper has access to the constant "x" of MyInterface, but it doesn't have access to the x variable of MyClass.

The statement System.out.print("q" + s + x); prints qw6 to the standard output, because x refers to the variable x of MyClass, which is 6.

The only correct answer is c.

Exercises

What happens if you remove the statement int x = 4; from the interface MyInterface?

What happens if you remove the statement int x = 6; from the class MyClass?

Assignment: A practical application of interfaces

In this example, employees and freelancers work for a particular employer. The employer withheld 30 % tax from the gross salary of the employees. The freelancers receive their payments based on their hourly rate and their working hours.

1. Create an interface with the name Payable with a method getSalary.
2. Create two classes namely Employee and Freelancer.
3. Both classes implement the interface Payable.

4. Overwrite the method getSalary in both classes.
5. Create a class named Test to test your code.
6. Create an employee object, that earns a monthly gross salary of $ 3000.
7. Create an object freelancer, who worked 140 hours for an hourly rate of $60.
8. Override the method getSalary in both classes to calculate how much the employer must pay each of them.

16. Casting

16.1. Casting Primitive Variables

Java supports implicit conversion to larger data types. However, casting to smaller data types can only be done explicitly. In some cases, it is necessary that the one variable is converted to another.

An example is dividing an int variable 31 by another int variable 2. The result is 15 while the desired result is 15.5. To achieve this, we use casting as follows.

int i = 31;
int i2 = 2;
int x = i / i2 = 15;

The int type is an integer without decimal places. In order to show the decimal value it is necessary to convert the result from int to a double type. We need to cast the int types to double types.

double d1 = i;
double d2 = i2;
double d3 = d1 / d2 = 15.5;

It is also possible to have the result in one line as follows.

double d4 = (**double**) i / i2;

Example 1
```
public class MyClass
{
  public static void main(String[] args)
  {
    int i = 31;
    int i2 = 2;
    int x = i / i2;
    double d1 = i;
    double d2 = i2;
    double d3 = d1 / d2;
    double d4 = (double) i / i2;
    System.out.println(x);
    System.out.println(d3);
    System.out.println(d4);
  }
}
```

This program writes the following to the standard output.
15
15.5
15.5

Other casting examples

short s = 20;
The following casting is valid, because int is larger than short:
int = 32 bits, short = 16 bit.

int i = s; // valid
int i2 = 200;

The following casting is invalid, because you cannot cast int directly to short.

short s2 = i2; // invalid

The following casting is valid. When converting from int to short an explicit casting is required. That can be done as follows.

short s3 = (**short**) i2; // valid

It is important to understand that int is 32 bits and short is 16 bits. The result is that 16 bits of the int variable are lost, because the value that is stored in an int is too big to fit in a short variable.

Example 2

```java
public class MyClass
{
   public static void main(String[] args)
   {
      short s = 20;
      int i = s; // valid
      int i2 = 200;
      short s2 = i2; // invalid
      short s3 = (short) i2; // valid
      System.out.println(s3);
   }
}
```

16.2. Casting objects

It is allowed in Java to put an object into a more general type or cast up the hierarchy implicitly. In the following example, the subclass Laptop has access to all the members of its superclass Computer, while the Computer class doesn't have access to all the members of the Laptop class.
The example below shows that the Laptop class extends the Computer class.
In our example, the Computer class has no access to the variable weight of the Laptop class, but the Laptop class does have access to the variable brand of the Computer class.
You can store a Computer object to a Laptop type reference without explicitly casting. If you try to store a Laptop object to a Computer type reference, explicit casting is required.
The following casting is valid.

Computer comp = **new** Laptop();
Laptop lap = (Laptop) comp;

The following casting is not valid.

Laptop lap = **new** Computer();

If we create an object of the class Computer the following casting causes error.

Computer comp2 = **new** Computer();
Laptop lap2 = (Laptop) comp2; // not valid

In the following way, it is possible to access the overridden methods in the subclass. The variables of the object comp depend on the reference of the object, but the methods depend on the object type that is created. See the following example.

Example 3
Computer.java
```java
public class Computer
{
  protected String brand = "Dell";
  protected double price = 200.0;;

  public double getPrice()
  {
    return price;
  }
}
```
Laptop.java
```java
public class Laptop extends Computer
{
  private double weight;

  public double getPrice()
  {
    return price - 20;
  }
  public static void main(String[] args)
  {
    Computer comp = new Laptop();
    Laptop lap = (Laptop) comp;
    Computer comp2 = new Computer();
    Laptop lap2 = (Laptop) comp2; // not valid
    System.out.println(comp.brand);
    System.out.println(comp.price);
    System.out.println(comp.getPrice());
  }
}
```

If this program is compiled and run, the following is written to the standard outpt.

Dell
200.0

180.0

Quiz 1: Casting primitive variables

What happens when the following program is compiled and run?

```java
public class MyClass
{
  public static void main(String[] args)
  {
    int i1 = 127;
    int i2 = 134;
    byte b1 = (byte) i1;
    byte b2 = (byte) i2;
    System.out.print(b1 + ", ");
    System.out.print(b2);
  }
}
```

Select the correct answer:

a This code writes to 127, 134 to the standard output.

b is The value of b1 is 127 , but the value of b2 is not printed as 134 .

Explanation

Byte is small and its value is between -128 and 127.

The value of b1 is 127 , but b2 is equal to 134 , which is greater than the maximum value of a byte .

The correct answer is b.

Exercises

Declare an int variable myInt.

Assign the value (i1 + i2) to the variable myInt.

Add a statement to your code to write the value of myInt to the standard output.

Declare a short variable with the name myShort .

Assign the value of i1 to myShort and run the program to see what happens.

Quiz 2: Casting primitive variables

What happens when the following program is compiled and run?

```java
public class MyClass
{
  public static void main(String[] args)
  {
    int i = 122;
    double d = i;
    System.out.print(d);
  }
}
```

Select the correct answer:

a This code writes 122.0 to the standard output.

b This code writes 122 to the standard output.

c This program cannot be compiled, because explicit casting is needed.

Explanation

The variable type double is 64 bits and this is larger than the int type which is 32 bits. In this case, explicit casting is not needed. The variable type double is a decimal type, therefore, is 122.0 written to the standard output.

The correct answer is a.

Exercises

Add the statement i = 187; add directly below the statement int

What is the value of the variable d ?

Run the program to get the answer to check.

Quiz 3: Casting objects

What happens when the following program is compiled and run?

```java
public class MySuper
{
  protected int i = 5;

  public int method()
  {
    return 2 * i;
  }
}


public class MySub extends MySuper
{
  int i = 3;

  public int method()
  {
    return 2 * i;
  }
  public static void main(String[] args)
  {
    MySuper s = new MySub();
    System.out.print(" " + s.i);
    System.out.print(" " + s.method());
  }
}
```

Select the correct answer:

a. This code writes "3 6" to the standard output.

b. This code writes "5 10" to the standard output.

c. This code writes "5 6" to the standard output.

d. This code writes "3 10" to the standard output.

e. This code does not compile.

Explanation

By upcasting the class MySuper to MySub, The casted object accesses the attributes of the superclass MySuper, but the overridden methods of the subclass MySub.

s.i = 5.

The statement s.method(); ivokes the method that overridden in the subclass.
s.method(); prints 2 * i = 3 * 2 = 6. to the standard output.

The correct answer is c.

Exercises

Add the statement MySub ms = s; directly below the statement MySuper s = new MySub();.
The statement of The first step causes an error. Try to solve the problem!
Add your own code to write the value of the variable i and the value that the method returns to the standard output.

Quiz 4: Casting objects
What happens when the following program is compiled and run?

```java
public class MySuper
{
  protected int x;

  MySuper()
  {
    x++;
    System.out.print("N");
  }
  int myMethod()
  {
    return x + 3;
  }
}

public class MySub extends MySuper
{
  MySub()
  {
    x += 2;
    System.out.print("P");
  }
  int myMethod()
  {
    return x + 4;
  }
  public static void main(String[] args)
  {
    MySuper ms = new MySub();
```

```
    System.out.print(ms.myMethod());
  }
}
```

Select the correct answer:

a. This code writes "NP7" to the standard output.

b. This code writes "NP5" to the standard output.

c. This code writes "P4" to the standard output.

d. This code writes "4" to the standard output.

e. This code writes "3" to the standard output.

f. This code does not compile.

Explanation

1. The statement MySuper ms = new MySub(); creates a new object of MySub, which calls first the the no-argument constructor of MySuper class. This adds one to the value of the variable x.
2. x = 0 + 1 = 1.
3. The statement System.out.print("N"); prints "N" to the standard output.

4. Creating the new object calls the no-argument constructor of MySub, which adds 2 to the value of x.
5. x = 1 + 2 = 3.
6. The statement System.out.print("P"); prints "P" to the standard output.

7. The statement System.out.print(ms.myMethod()); refers to the overridden method in the class MySub.

8. The method myMethod return x + 4; adds 4 to the value of x.
9. x = 3 + 4 = 7.
10. The result is: NP7

The correct answer is a.

Exercises

Replace the statement MySuper ms = new MySub(); in the main method with MySuper ms = new MySuper(); What would be the result of executing the program?

Quiz 5: Casting objects and overriding methods

What happens when the following program is compiled and run?

```
public class MySuper
{
  public MySuper()
  {
    System.out.print("m");
  }
  public void method()
  {
    System.out.print("s");
  }
  public void method(int i)
  {
    method();
```

```
    System.out.print("k" + i);
  }
}
public class MySub extends MySuper
{
  public void method()
  {
    System.out.print("t");
  }
  public static void main(String[] args)
  {
    MySuper ms = new MySub();
    ms.method(3);
  }
}
```

Select the correct answer:
a. This code writes "msk3" to the standard output.
b. This code writes "mtk3" to the standard output.
c. This code writes "tk3" to the standard output.
d. This code writes "mst" to the standard output.
e. This code does not compile.

Explanation
The statement MySuper ms = new MySub(); calls the no-argument constructor of MySuper, which print "m" to the standard output.
The statement ms.method(3); invokes the method of int parameter which, invokes the no-parameter method. The method is overridden in the class MySub, and that is why it prints "t" to the standard output.
The statement System.out.print("k"+i), prints "k3" to the standard output, because the parameter i is equal to 3.
The result is: mtk3.

The correct answer is b.

Exercises
Replace the statement MySuper ms = new MySub(); in the main method with the statment MySuper ms = new MySuper();.
What is the output if you execute the program?

Assignment: Working with Java API documentation

1. The class ArrayList implements the interface List .
2. Create a class with with the name MyList .
3. Declare two objects in MyList as follows.
   a. List<String> list = new ArrayList<String>();
   b. ArrayList<String> aList = new ArrayList<String>();
4. Try to invoke the method clone. Use the object names list and aList .
5. Why the object list does not have access to the method clone?

17. Nested Classes

A nested class is a member of another class, which is known as enclosing class or an outer class.
The two main categories of nested classes are:

17.1. Static Nested Classes

A static nested class is directly connected to its outer class, but it does not have a direct access to the instance members of its outer class. A static nested class can access the members of its outer class through an object.

17.2. Inner Classes

Inner classes have direct access to all members of their outer classes, even if they are declared private.
The nested class and its outer class have a strong relationship, because their existence depends on each other. An example is a building and its rooms. The rooms of a building can not exist without the building in which they exist. Another example is the relationship between a body and a heart. To create an object of a nested class, An object of the outer class must be created.

17.3. Advantages Of Nested Classes

Nested classes are only useful for their outer classes, therefore, it is logical to keep them together. The definition of a nested class within an outer class makes the code easier to maintain.
Nested classes are hidden for other classes.

17.4. Outer Classes

An outer class can only be declared public or package (see the chapter Access Modifiers).
An outer class does not have a direct access to the members of its nested classes.

17.5. Static Nested Classes

A static nested class is associated with its outer class.
A static nested class does not have a direct access to the members of its outer class, but it has access to those members through an object.
You can access static nested classes through the name of its outer class.

The creation of an object of a static nested class
Outer.Nest nest = **new** Outer.Nest();

Outer :   the outer class
Nest :   the static nested class
nest :   an object of the nested class

17.6. Inner classes Associated

An inner class is associated with an instance of the outer class.
An inner class has a direct access to the members of the object of the outer class.

You can't create an object of an inner class without creating an object of the outer class.

The creation of an object of an inner class
You can create an object of an inner class by creating an object of the outer class as following.

Outer out = **new** Outer();
Inner in = out.**new** Inner();

Outer: the outer class
Inner: the inner class
out: an object of the outer class
in   an object of the inner class

You can also create an object of an inner class in a single line.

Outer.Inner in = **new** Outer().**new** Inner();

Example
```java
public class Face
{
  private String faceShape = "Round";
  private String skinColor = "Tinted";

  public void printInfo()
  {
    System.out.println("Face shape:      " + faceShape);
    System.out.println("Skin color:      " + skinColor);
  }

  class Eye
  {
    String color = "Brown";
    String leftStrength = "- 2";
    String rightStrength = "-1.5";

    public void printInfo()
    {
      System.out.println("Eye color:       " + color);
      System.out.println("Left Strength:   " + leftStrength);
      System.out.println("Right Strength:  " + rightStrength);
    }
  }

  public static void main(String[] args)
  {
    Face face = new Face();
    Eye eye = face.new Eye();
    face.printInfo();
    eye.printInfo();
```

```
    }
}
```

Quiz 1: Access of Inner class to the members of its outer class

What happens when the following program is compiled and run?

```java
public class Outer
{
  int x;

  Outer()
  {
    x += 4;
  }

  class Inner
  {
    int x;

    private void methodA()
    {
      x++;
      System.out.print(x);
    }
  }

  public static void main(String[] args)
  {
    Inner inner = new Outer().new Inner();
    inner.methodA();
  }
}
```

Select the correct answer:

a. This program writes "0" to the standard output.

b. This program writes "4" to the standard output.

c. This program writes "5" to the standard output.

d. This program writes "1" to the standard output.

e. This program does not compile.

Explanation

The statement Inner inner = new Outer().new Inner(); calls the no-argument constructor of the outer class, which adds 4 to the value of the variable "x" of the outer class.

However, the methodA writes the value of the variable x of the inner class, which is "0".

The statement x++ adds one to the value of x, and that is why this code writes "1" to the standard output.

The correct answer is d.

Exercises

What is written to the standard output if you change the name of the variable x of the inner class to y?

Quiz 2: A simple inner class

What happens when the following program is compiled and run?

```java
public class Outer
{
  private int a = 2;

  Outer()
  {
    a += 4;
  }

  class Inner
  {
    Inner()
    {
      a++;
    }
  }

  public static void main(String[] args)
  {
    Outer outer = new Outer();
    Inner inner = outer.new Inner();
    System.out.print(outer.a);
  }
}
```

Select the correct answer:

a. This program writes "2" to the standard output.

b. This program writes "7" to the standard output.

c. This program writes "6" to the standard output.

d. This program writes "3" to the standard output.

e. This program does not compile.

Explanation

The statement Outer outer = new Outer(); calls the no-argument constructor of the outer class, which adds 4 to the value of the varaible a.

a = 2 + 4 = 6

The statement Inner inner = outer.new Inner(); calls the no-argument constructor of the inner class which increments the value of a by one.

A = 6 + 1 = 7.

The correct answer is b.

Exercises

What is the output if you change the initial value of the variable ' a' to 5?

Compile and run the program to test the result.

Quiz 3: Outer class one-argument constructor

What happens when the following program is compiled and run?

```java
class Outer
{
    private int x = 2;

    Outer()
    {
        this(3);
        x++;
    }
    Outer(int i)
    {
        x += i;
        System.out.print(x);
    }

    class Inner
    {
        private void methodA()
        {
            x -= 3;
            System.out.print(x);
        }
    }

    public static void main(String[] args)
    {
        Outer.Inner inner = new Outer().new Inner();
        inner.methodA();
    }
}
```

Select the correct answer:

a. This program writes "63" to the standard output.

b. This program writes "5" to the standard output.

c. This program writes "53" to the standard output.

d. This program writes "52" to the standard output.

e. This program does not compile.

Explanation

The statement Inner inner = new Outer().new Inner(); calls the no-argument constructor of the outer class.

The no-argument constructor calls the one-argument constructor of the outer class, which increment the value of x by 3.

x = 2 + 3 = 5.

The statement System.out.print(x); prints 5 to the standard output.

x++; increments the value of x by one.

x = 5 + 1 = 6.

The statement inner.method(); invokes the method methodA, which decrements the value of x by 3.

x = 6 - 3 = 3

The statement System.out.print(x); prints "3" to the standard output.

The correct answer is c.

Exercises

What is the output of this program if you replace the statement Outer.Inner inner = new Outer().new Inner(); with the statement Outer.Inner inner = new Outer(7).new Inner();?

Quiz 4: A static nested class

What happens when the following program is compiled and run?

```java
class Outer
{
    static int x = 3;

    Outer()
    {
        x += 4;
    }

    static class Nested
    {
        Nested()
        {
            x += 2;
        }
        int method(int i)
        {
            System.out.print(x);
            return i + x;
        }
    }

    public static void main(String[] args)
    {
        Outer.Nested instance = new Outer.Nested();
        System.out.print(instance.method(2));
    }
}
```

Select the correct answer:

a. This program writes "1113" to the standard output.

b. This program writes "7" to the standard output.

c. This program writes "11" to the standard output.

d. This program writes "57" to the standard output.

e. This program does not compile.

Explanation

The statement Nested instance = new Outer.Nested(); calls the no-argument constructor of the nested class.

The constructor increments the value of x by two.

x = 3 + 2 = 5;

The statement System.out.print(instance.method(2)); invokes the one parameter method.

The statement System.out.print(x); prints the last value of x to the standard output, which is 5.

The statement System.out.print(instance.method(2)); prints the number that is returned by the method.

i + x = 2 + 5 = 7;

The correct answer is d.

Exercises

Add the statement Outer outer = new Outer(); as first statement of the main method. What would be the output if you compile and run the program?

Assignment: Working with Java API documentation

1. Create a class called Car. We need to know about the cars, the brand, the year of manufacture and the license plate.
2. We need further to know information about the engines of the cars as: engine code and the fuel.
3. Write a program which prints all the information about the cars to the standard output.
4. By executing your program something like below would be printed to the standard output.

Brand: BMW
Year of manufacture: 2016
License plate: XN-45-489
Engine code: N45B20A
Fuel: Petrol

18. Exceptions

An exception is an abnormal condition, which might occur during the execution of a program.

The exception objects in Java contain information about the errors. There are two types of Exceptions: **checked** and **unchecked** Exceptions.

The following keywords are used to handle exceptions: **try, catch, throw, throws** and **finally.**

Exceptions might cause by several reasons, for example, entering letters in a field that is designed for calculating numbers, trying to access the seventh element of an array of five-elements or trying to access a file, which doesn't exist.

All exceptions in Java are derived from the class Throwable. The following methods of the class Throwable are used to get information about the cause of the errors.

Diagram 1 shows the Exception class hierarchy in Java.

See for further information about the class Throwable the online documentation of the Java standard API.

Method	Return type	Description
printStackTrace()	void	Write the possible errors to the standard error-stream.
getMessage()	String	returns the message as a String.

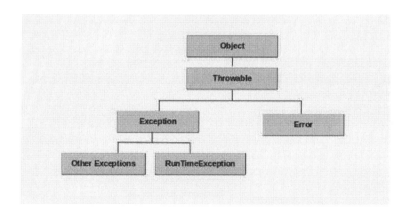

Diagram 1

The two subclasses of Exception: RunTimeException (unchecked) and Other Exceptions (checked).

18.1. RuntimeException (Unchecked)

The RuntimeException is unchecked and it is not enforced by the Java compiler. Programmers are free to ignore the RunTimeException. However, it is wise to handle these exceptions, so that the users receives a message that explains the cause of the exception.

Examples of unchecked exceptions:

ArithmeticException

Divide-by-0.

ClassCastException

By illegal casting.

IndexArrayOutOfBoundsException

If you try to access element 8 of an array of 7 elements.

NullPointerException

When trying to access a member of an object reference before the object is created.

18.2. Other Exceptions (Checked)

The checked exceptions cannot be ignored; they should be handled by programmers. Examples of these are: the network connection is not found, a file is not found and so on.

18.3. The Try-Catch Block

In the following program, we divide a number by 0 without handling the exception.

Example 1

```java
public class MyClass
{
  public static int division(int numerator, int denominator)
  {
    System.out.println("The method division()");
    return numerator / denominator;
  }
  public static void printResult(int numerator, int denominator)
  {
    int average = division(numerator, denominator);
    System.out.println("Average = " + average);
    System.out.println("End printResult()");
  }
  public static void main(String[] args)
  {
    printResult(25, 0);
    System.out.println("End main()");
  }
}
```

Explanation

1. The statement printingResult (25, 0); in the main method invokes the method printResult.
2. The statement int average = division(numerator, denominator); calls the method division()
3. The statement System.out.print("The method of division()"); writes the text to The method
4. the division sign() to the standard output.
5. The statement return numerator/denominator calculates 25 / 0 and here is exception occur, because
6. the denominator is equal to zero. The program cannot go further because we haven' t handled the exception.
7. The output of the program in the console window looks like the following.

division() Exception in thread "main"

The method division()
Exception in thread "main" java.lang.ArithmeticException: / by zero
        at _17_exceptions.ex._01.MyClass.division(MyClass.java:8)
        at _17_exceptions.ex._01.MyClass.printResult(MyClass.java:12)
        at _17_exceptions.ex._01.MyClass.main(MyClass.java:18)

It is important that programmers handle this kind of exceptions and providing the users with the correct message if an error occurs. You can handle the exception with a try-catch block, see the following example.

Example 2

```java
public class MyClass
{
  public static int division(int numerator, int denominator)
  {
    System.out.println("The method division()");
    return numerator / denominator;
  }
  public static void printResult(int numerator, int denominator)
  {
    try
    {
      int average = division(numerator, denominator);
      System.out.println("Average = " + average);
    }
    catch (ArithmeticException ae)
    {
      System.out.println(ae);
      System.out.println("Handeling the exception");
    }
    System.out.println("End printResult()");
  }
  public static void main(String[] args)
  {
    printResult(25, 0);
    System.out.println("End main()");
  }
}
```

Explanation

The statement printingResult (25, 0); invokes the method printResult.
The statement int average = division(numerator, denominator); calls the method division().

The statement System.out.print("The method of division()"); writes the text "The method the division()" to the standard output.
The statement return numerator / denominator calculates 25 / 0, and here the exception occurs because the denominator is equal to zero.

The exception is in the first line of the try-block, and the block is further ignored.

The exception is caught in the catch block.

The statement System.out.println(ae); writes the exception type and its cause to the standard output.

The program writes further the texts End printResult() and also End main() to the standard output as follows.

The method division()

java.lang.ArithmeticException: / by zero

Handeling the exception

End printResult()

End main()

Exercises

Replace the statement printResult(25, 0); with the statement printResult(25, 5);

Compile and run the program to see what happens.

Answer

In this case, we divide the number 25 by 5, that is why the try-block is executed, and the catch block is ignored. The program writes the following to the standard output.

The method division()

Average = 5

End printResult()

End main()

You can use as many catch-blocks behind each other as you want, but you need to keep in mind the order of the exceptions.

In the following example, the catch block Exception is under the catch-block IndexOutOfBoundsException, because the class Exception is higher than the class IndexOutOfBoundsException in the hierarchy of the exception classes. For the same reason, the catch block of IndexOutOfBoundsException is under the catch-block of ArrayIndexOutOfBoundsException. See Diagram 2.

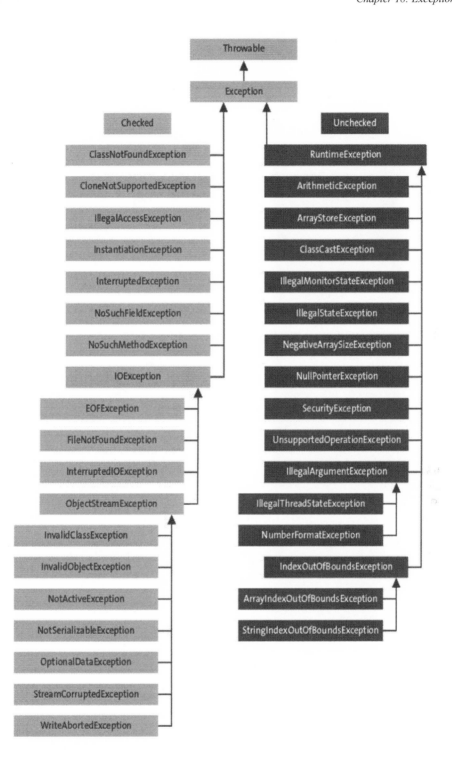

Diagram 2

Example 3
```java
public class MyClass
{
  public static void main(String[] args)
  {
    try
    {
      // A code which may cause an exception
    }
    catch (ArrayIndexOutOfBoundsException ae)
    {
      // catch the exception ArrayIndexOutOfBoundsException
    }
    catch (IndexOutOfBoundsException ae)
    {
      // catch the exception IndexOutOfBoundsException
    }
    catch (Exception e)
    {
      // catch all other possible exceptions
    }
  }
}
```

18.4. The Finally-Block

The finally-block follows either the try or the catch block, and it is always executed whether exceptions occurs or not. Finally is used for example to close a network connection or to close a file. See the following example.

Example 4
```java
public class MyClass
{
  public static int division(int numerator, int denominator)
  {
    System.out.println("The method division()");
    return numerator / denominator;
  }
  public static void printResult(int numerator, int denominator)
  {
    try
    {
      int average = division(numerator, denominator);
      System.out.println("Average = " + average);
    }
    catch (ArithmeticException ae)
    {
      System.out.println(ae);
```

```
      System.out.println("Handeling the exception");
    }
    finally
    {
      System.out.println("Finally block is always executed");
    }
    System.out.println("End printResult()");
  }
  public static void main(String[] args)
  {
    printResult(25, 0);
    System.out.println("End main()");
  }
}
```

Explanation

The difference between this example and example 2 is that in this example, the block finally is always executed.
This code writes the following to the standard output.

The method division()
java.lang.ArithmeticException: / by zero
Handeling the exception
Finally block is always executed
End printResult()
End main()

18.5. The Keywords Throw And Throws

A Java code can throw an exception with the keywords throw and throws. You can catch these exceptions
with a catch block. The keyword throws is used in the header of the methods, but the keyword throw is
used in the body of the methods. See examples 5 and 6.
In the following program, a new object ArithmeticException("Division by zero") is thrown if the
denominator of the fraction is equal to 0.

Example 5

```
public class MyClass
{
  public static int division(int numerator, int denominator)
  {
    System.out.println("The method division(()");
    if (denominator == 0)
    {
      throw new ArithmeticException("Division by zero");
    }
    return numerator / denominator;
  }
  public static void printResult(int numerator, int denominator)
  {
    try
    {
```

```
      int average = division(numerator, denominator);
      System.out.println("Average = " + average);
    }
    catch (ArithmeticException ae)
    {
      System.out.println(ae);
      System.out.println("Exception is handled in the printResult()");
    }
  }
  public static void main(String[] args)
  {
    printResult(25, 0);
    System.out.println("End main()");
  }
}
```

Explanation

This example is similar to example 2, except that here the control
if(denominator == 0) is used. If the denominator is equal to 0, the exception ArithmeticException is thrown.
In the method printResult, the exception is caught. We have also passed a customized exception text " Division by
zero" to the method. This replaces the default message "/ by zero" .
This code writes the following to the standard output.

The method division(()
java.lang.ArithmeticException: Division by zero
Exception is handled in the printResult()
End main()

18.6. Create And Throw Your Own Exception Class

In the following example, a customized exception class MyException is created. This class is a checked
exception because it is a subclass of the class Exception.
If an exception occurs, you can show your own customized text instead of the default text.

Example 6

```
public class MyException extends Exception
{
  MyException(String str)
  {
    super(str);
  }
}
public class MyClass
{
  public static int division(int numerator, int denominator) throws MyException
  {
    System.out.println("The method division(()");
    if (denominator == 0)
    {
      throw new MyException("Division by zero");
```

```
    }
    return numerator / denominator;
  }
  public static void printResult(int numerator, int denominator)
  {
    try
    {
      int average = division(numerator, denominator);
      System.out.println("Average = " + average);
    }
    catch (MyException me)
    {
      System.out.println(me);
      System.out.println("Exception is handled in the printResult()");
    }
  }
  public static void main(String[] args)
  {
    printResult(25, 0);
    System.out.println("End main()");
  }
}
```

This code writes the following to the standard output.

The method division(()
_17_exceptions.ex._06.MyException: Division by zero

Exception is handled in the printResult()
End main()

18.7. Error Class

The Error class is a subclass of the class Throwable. Errors can occur at runtime and programmers in most cases do not have control over them. Examples are: StackOverflowError, OutOfMemoryError, and UnknowError.

Quiz 1: Unchecked exception (RunTimeException)

What happens when the following program is compiled and run?

```
public class MyClass
{
  public void method()
  {
    try
    {
      System.out.print("x");
      int x = Integer.parseInt("hi");
```

```java
      System.out.print("y");
    }
    catch (NumberFormatException e)
    {
      System.out.print("z");
    }
  }
  public static void main(String[] args)
  {
    MyClass mc = new MyClass();
    mc.method();
  }
}
```

Select the correct answer:
a. This program writes "xyz" to the standard output.
b. This program writes "xz" to the standard output.
c. This program writes "xy" to the standard output.
d. This program writes "yz" to the standard output.
e. This program does not compile.

Explanation
The statement "System.out.print("x");" in the try block prints "x" to the standard output.
The statement "int x = Integer.parseInt("hi");" tries to parse the string argument as an integer, which throws a NumberFormatException. The program jumps to the catch block.
The statement "System.out.print("z");" prints "z" to the standard output.

The correct answer is b.

Exercises
Use Java standard API and Search for the class Integer. You can find the link to the Java standard API at the beginning of this book.

Find the method paraseInt("String str"), and read its description.
Replace the statement int x = Integer.parseInt("hi"); with int x = Integer.parseInt("38");.
What is the output? Compile and run the program to test your expected result.

Quiz 2: Handling exceptions and the finally block

What happens when the following program is compiled and run?

```java
public class MyClass
{
  public void method()
  {
    try
    {
```

```
      int[] intArray = new int[5];
      int z = intArray[6];
      System.out.print("w");
    }
    catch (ArithmeticException e)
    {
      System.out.print("x");
    }
    catch (ArrayIndexOutOfBoundsException e)
    {
      System.out.print("y");
    }
    finally
    {
      System.out.print("z");
    }
  }
  public static void main(String[] args)
  {
    MyClass mc = new MyClass();
    mc.method();
  }
}
```

Select the correct answer:

a. This program writes "wz" to the standard output.

b. This program writes "yz" to the standard output.

c. This program writes "wyz" to the standard output.

d. This program writes "xz" to the standard output.

e. This program does not compile.

Explanation

The statement "int z = intArray[6];" tries to access the sixth element of the array intArray, which doesn't exist.

This exception ArrayIndexOutOfBoundsException occurs and the statement System.out.print("y"), prints "y" to the standard output.

The finally-block is always executed.

The statement System.out.print("z"), prints "z" to the standard output.

The correct answer is b.

Exercises

What happens if the finally-block is removed from the code?

Compile and run the program to check out your expectation.

Quiz 3: Unchecked exceptions and the finally block

What happens when the following program is compiled and run?

```java
public class MyClass
{
  String str;

  public void method()
  {
    try
    {
      str.substring(1);
      System.out.print("s");
    }
    catch (NullPointerException e)
    {
      System.out.print("x");
    }
    catch (Exception e)
    {
      System.out.print("y");
    }
    finally
    {
      System.out.print("z");
    }
  }
  public static void main(String[] args)
  {
    MyClass mc = new MyClass();
    mc.method();
  }
}
```

Select the correct answer:
a. This program writes "xz" to the standard output.
b. This program writes "syz" to the standard output.
c. This program writes "yz" to the standard output.
d. This program writes "z" to the standard output.
e. This program does not compile.

Explanation
The String str is a reference to an object, which is not created.
String str = null;
By trying to access a substring of str, a NullPointerException occurs.
The statement System.out.print("x"), prints x to the standard output.
The finally block always executed.

The statement System.out.print("z"), prints z to the standard output.

The correct answer is a.

Exercises
Assign the value of "Boris" to the variable str.
What would be the output of the program?
Compile and run the code to test your expected result.

Quiz 4: Handling the exception of divided by zero
What happens when the following program is compiled and run?

```java
public class MyClass
{
  int x;

  public void method()
  {
    try
    {
      int i = 2 / x;
      System.out.print("a");
    }
    catch (NullPointerException n)
    {
      System.out.print("b");
    }
    catch (ArithmeticException e)
    {
      System.out.print("d");
    }
    finally
    {
      System.out.print("f");
    }
  }
  public static void main(String[] args)
  {
    MyClass mc = new MyClass();
    mc.method();
  }
}
```

Select the correct answer:
a. This program writes "df" to the standard output.
b. This program writes "ab" to the standard output.
c. This program writes "bf" to the standard output.

d. This program writes "f" to the standard output.

e. This program does not compile.

Explanation

The catch block NullPointerException doesn't catch the exception because dividing by zero is an ArithmeticException.

The catch block ArithmeticException is executed and prints "d" to the standard output.

The finally block is always executed, and it prints "f" to the standard output.

The correct answer is a.

Exercises

1. Assign the value of 20 to the variable x.
2. What is the output if you compile and run the code?
3. Execute the program to test your answer.

Quiz 5: Which exception is caught?

What happens when the following program is compiled and run?

```java
public class MyClass
{
  StringBuffer sb;
  int z;

  public void myMethod()
  {
    try
    {
      z = 5 / 0;
      sb.append("s");
    }
    catch (NullPointerException e)
    {
      System.out.print("n");
    }
    catch (ArithmeticException ae)
    {
      System.out.print("a");
    }
  }
  public static void main(String[] args)
  {
    MyClass mc = new MyClass();
    mc.myMethod();
  }
}
```

Select the correct answer:

a. This code writes n to the standard output.

b. This code writes an to the standard output.

c. This code writes a to the standard output.

d. This code writes na to the standard output.

e. This code cannot be compiled.

Explanation

The two statements of the try block cause exceptions, but the first statement is first executed. The first statement causes ArithmetcException , therefore, is the second catch-block is executed.
The statement System.out.print("a"); writes a to the standard output.

The correct answer is c.

Exercises

1. What is the result of the execution of the program if the position of the statements within the try block is changed as following?
   sb.append("s");
   z = 5/0;
2. Compile and run the program to check out your answer.

Quiz 6: Throwing an exception

What happens when the following program is compiled and run?

```java
public class MyClass
{
  static String str = "";

  static void calculate(int x, int y)
  {
    str += "A";
    if (y == 0)
    {
      throw new ArithmeticException();
    }
    int z = x / y;
    str += "B";
  }
  public static void main(String[] args)
  {
    try
    {
      str += "C";
      calculate(10, 0);
      str += "D";
    }
    catch (ArithmeticException e)
```

```
    {
      str += "E";
    }
    catch (ArrayIndexOutOfBoundsException ae)
    {
      str += "F";
    }
    System.out.println(str);
  }
}
```

Select the correct answer:

a. This code writes ABE to the standard output.

b. This code writes CAF to the standard output.

c. This code writes CAE to the standard output.

d. This code writes ABCD to the standard output.

e. This code cannot be compiled.

Explanation

The statement str += "C"; inside the try-block adds the letter C to the String str.

The statement calculate(10, 0); calls the method calculate.

The statement str += "A" within the method calculate adds the letter A to the String str .

The statement if(y == 0) returns true and the exception ArithmeticException is thrown.

The catch block of the exception, ArithmeticException is caught.

The statement str += "E"; adds the letter E to the String str .

The correct answer is c.

Exercises

What is written to the standard output if the statement throw new ArithmeticException(); is replaced with the statement throw new ArrayIndexOutOfBoundsException(); ?

Compile and run the program to check.

Quiz 7: The keyword throw

What happens when the following program is compiled and run?

```
public class MyClass
{
  public static void test(String str)
  {
    if (str == null)
    {
      throw new NullPointerException();
    }
    else
    {
      throw new RuntimeException();
```

```java
      }
    }
    public static void main(String[] args)
    {
      try
      {
        System.out.print("A");
        test("");
      }
      catch (NullPointerException e)
      {
        System.out.print("B");
      }
      catch (Exception e)
      {
        System.out.print("C");
      }
      finally
      {
        System.out.print("D");
      }
    }
}
```

Select the correct answer:

a. This code writes the AD to the standard output.

b. This code writes ABCD to the standard output.

c. This code writes AC to the standard output.

d. This code writes ACD to the standard output.

e. This code cannot be compiled.

Explanation

The statement System.out.print("A"); within the try-block writes A to the standard output

The method test("") is invoked.

If the statement if(str == null) returns true, the exception NullPointerException is caught, otherwise a RuntimeException.

The parameter of the method test("") is not equal to null , therefore, the RuntimeException is thrown.

The catch block Exception is higher in the exception class hierarchy than the RuntimeException, which is why it is caught. See diagram 2 for the exception class hierarchy.

The statement System.out.print("C"); writes the letter C to the standard output.

The finally block is always executed, therefore, the letter D is also written to the standard output.

The correct answer is d.

Exercises

1. What would be written to the standard output if the statement test(""); within the try-block is replaced by the statement test(null);?

2. Compile and run the program to check out your answer.

Assignment: Create your own exception class

In the following program, a customized exception class is created with the name MyException. The method getMovie(int movieIndex) is invoked in the main method, but the body of the method is missing.

Write the missing statements in the body of the method getMovie.
If the movieIndex is greater than 5, the program should write "the movie does not exist". Throw the exception MyException.
If a movieIndex exist, the program should write the title of the movie to the standard output. For index 0 the program writes The Godfather to the standard output. For index 1 the program writes Titanic to the standard output, and so on.
Test your program whether it works properly.
Replace in the catch block, the statement System.out.print(me.getMessage()); with the statement me.printStackTrace();
Run the program to see the difference between the methods getMessage and printStackTrace .

```java
public class MyException extends Exception
{
  public MyException(String message)
  {
    super(message);
  }
}

import java.util.ArrayList;

public class Test
{
  private static ArrayList<String> movieList = new ArrayList<String>();

  public static void populateList()
  {
    movieList.add("The Godfather");
    movieList.add("Titanic");
    movieList.add("Dances with Wolves");
    movieList.add("The Pianist");
    movieList.add("Wall Street");
    movieList.add("Amadeus");
  }
  public static String getMovie(int movieIndex) throws MyException
  {
    // the body
  }
  public static void main(String args[])
  {
```

```
    populateList();
    try
    {
      String movie = getMovie(15);
      System.out.print("The movie title is: " + movie);
    }
    catch (MyException me)
    {
      System.out.print(me.getMessage());
      // me.printStackTrace();
    }
  }
}
```

The Answers Of The Exercises

1. Answers Data Object Oriented Programming

Quiz 1

```java
class Car
{
  String brand;
  int mileage;
  double price;
  String color;

  public static void main(String[] args)
  {
    Car car1 = new Car();
    Car car2 = new Car();
    Car car3 = new Car();

    car1.brand = "Volkswagen";
    car1.mileage = 4000;
    car1.price = 4500.75;
    car1.color = "black";

    car2.brand = "Mazda";
    car2.mileage = 2000;
    car2.price = 3500.65;
    car2.color = "red";

    car3.brand = "Nissan";
    car3.mileage = 7000;
    car3.price = 6500.25;
    car3.color = "white";

    System.out.println("Brand 1: " +car1.brand +
  ", color: " + car1.color);
    System.out.println("Brand 2: " +car2.brand +
  ", color: " + car2.color);
    System.out.println("Brand 3: " +car3.brand +
  ", color: " + car3.color);
  }
}
```

Quiz 2

```java
class Animal
{
  String name;
  String sort;

  public static void main(String[] args)
  {
    Animal animal1 = new Animal();
    Animal animal2 = new Animal();
    Animal animal3 = new Animal();

    animal1.name = "Tiger";
    animal1.sort = "predator ";

    animal2.name = "Dog";
    animal2.sort = "pet ";

    animal3.name = "Cow";
    animal3.sort = "farm animal";

    System.out.println(animal1.name +",
  "+animal1.sort);
    System.out.println(animal2.name +",
  "+animal2.sort);
    System.out.println(animal3.name +",
  "+animal3.sort);
  }
}
```

Quiz 3

```java
class Computer
{
  String brand;
  int hardDisk;
  int ram;

  public static void main(String[] args)
  {
    Computer comp = new Computer();
    Computer myComputer = new Computer();
    Computer thisComputer = new Computer();
    Computer computer = new Computer();

    myComputer.brand = "HP";
    myComputer.hardDisk = 120;
    myComputer.ram = 8;

    System.out.println("Brand:      " +myComputer.brand);
    System.out.println("Harde disk:  " +myComputer.hardDisk + "
  GB");
    System.out.println("RAM:        " +myComputer.ram + " GB");
  }
}
```

2. Answers Data Types and Variables

Quiz 1

```
class Worker
{
  boolean isMarried;
  int age = 29;
  long bankAccount = 6552;
  double wage = 110.30;
  char gender = 'm'; // female: f, male: m

  public static void main(String[] args)
  {
    Worker wk = new Worker();

    System.out.print(wk.age + ", ");
    System.out.print(wk.bankAccount + ", ");
    System.out.print(wk.wage + ", ");
    System.out.print(wk.isMarried + ", ");
    System.out.println(wk.gender);
    // Answer
    System.out.print("Het antwoord: ");
    boolean isForeigner = true;
    System.out.print(isForeigner);
  }
}
```

1. A practical variable choice is boolean because the value of the variable isForeigner is either true (foreigner) or false (not foreigner).
2. To avoid unnecessary work, the variable "isForeigner" should be true by default. The reason is that most of the workers are foreigners.

Quiz 2

```
class MyVariable
{
  byte b = 122;
  short s;
  float f1 = 3.50f;
  float f2 = 43.9f;
  double d = 335.35;
  char myChar = 'Q';

  public static void main(String[] args)
  {
    MyVariable mv = new MyVariable();

    System.out.print(mv.b + ", ");
    // System.out.print(myChar + ", ");
    System.out.print(mv.s + ", ");
    System.out.print(mv.f1 + ", ");
    // System.out.print(myChar + ", ");
    System.out.print(mv.f2 + ", ");
    System.out.println(mv.d);
    // Answer
    System.out.print(mv.myChar);
  }
}
```

Quiz 3

```
class MyClass
{
  int i;
  double d;
  boolean b;

  public static void main(String[] args)
  {
    MyClass mc = new MyClass();

    System.out.print(mc.i + ", ");
    System.out.print(mc.d + ", ");
    System.out.println(mc.b);
    // Answer
    double myVar = 1344.98;
    char myVar2 = 'g';
    int myVar3 = 766;

    System.out.print("The answer: ");
    System.out.print(myVar + ", ");
    System.out.print(myVar2 + ", ");
    System.out.print(myVar3);
  }
}
```

1. The value of 1344.98 is a floating point type, it should be double or float.
2. The value of the "g" is a character type, it should be char.
3. The value of 766 is an integer type, it should be short, int or long.

Quiz 4

```
class MyClass
{
  int i1 = 7;
  int i2 = 12;

  public static void main(String[] args)
  {
    MyClass mc = new MyClass();

    mc.i1 = 9;
    mc.i2 = 8;
    mc.i1 = mc.i1 - 3;
    mc.i2 = mc.i2 + mc.i1;

    System.out.print(mc.i1 + ", ");
    System.out.print(mc.i2 + " ");
  }
}
```

3. The statement "i1 = 9" is under the previous initial value of i1, and that is why the value i1 = i1 - 3 = 9 - 3 = 6.

The statement "i2 = 8" is under the previous initial value of i2. The new value of i2 is 8.

i2 = i2 + i1 = 8 + 6 = 14.

3. Answers Operators

Quiz 1

```
class Calculate
{
  public static void main(String[] args)
  {
    int x = 20;
    int y = 5;
    int z = 3;
    double d = 2.2;
    double d2 = 3.7;

    System.out.print(x / y + ", ");
    System.out.print(x * z + ", ");
    System.out.print(x + y - z + ", ");
    System.out.print(x / y + z * 2 + ", ");
    System.out.println(d2 - d);
    // Answer
    System.out.print("The answer is: ");
    System.out.print(x * y / 10 + ", ");
    System.out.print(2 * d2 + 2.5 + ", ");
    System.out.print(z * 3 - 6);
  }
}
```

The answer is: 10, 9.9, 3

Quiz 2

```
class MyClass
{
  public static void main(String[] args)
  {
    System.out.print(21 % 7 + ", ");
    System.out.print(12 % 5 + ", ");
    System.out.println(23 % 6);
    // Answer
    System.out.print("The answer is: ");
    System.out.print(44 % 10 + ", ");
    System.out.print(7 % 2 + ", ");
    System.out.print(30 % 3);
  }
}
```

The answer is: 4, 1, 0

Quiz 3

```
class MyClass
{
  public static void main(String[] args)
  {
    int x = 4;
    int y = 6;

    x--;
    y++;
    // Answer
    System.out.print("The answer is: ");
    x++;
    System.out.print(x + ", " + y);
```

```
    // x++;
  }
}
```

1. The value of x is incremented by one after it is written to the standard output. The result remains the same.

The answer: 3, 7

2. The value of x is incremented by one before its value is written to the standard output. This will change the result.

The answer is: 4, 7

Quiz 4

```
class MyClass
{
  public static void main(String[] args)
  {
    int x = 15;
    int y = 8;
    int z = 3;

    if (x == z)
    {
      System.out.print("N");
    }
    if (x >= y)
    {
      System.out.print("O");
      System.out.print("Z");
    }
    if (x <= z)
    {
      System.out.print("P");
    }
    if (z > y)
    {
      System.out.print("Q");
    }
    if (y != z)
    {
      System.out.print("R");
    }
  }
}
```

By assigning the value 15 to the variable x, the statement if(x >= y) returns true.
The statement if(x == z) returns false.
The result is that OZR is written to the standard output.

Quiz 5

```
class MyClass
{
  public static void main(String[] args)
  {
    boolean isDefect = false;
    int x = 1;
```

```
    int y = 7;
    int z = 9;

    if (x < y && x > 1)
    {
      System.out.print("N");
    }
    if (z > y || x > y)
    {
      System.out.print("O");
    }
    if (!isDefect)
    {
      System.out.print("P");
    }
  }
}
```

1. If isDefect is false then the last statement if(! isDefect) returns true, and the program writes also P to the standard output.
2. If x is equal to 1, the statement if(x < y && x > 1) returns false. In this case x is not greater than one.
3. The result is that the code writes OP to the standard output.

Quiz 6

```
class MyClass
{
  public static void main(String[] args)
  {
    boolean isOld = true;
    int x = 5;
    int y = 14;
    int z = 17;

    if (y > x && z > y && (x + 12) >= z)
    {
      System.out.print("P");
    }
    if (x >= 6 || z <= y || z <= 18)
    {
      System.out.print("Q");
    }
    if (!isOld || y > z)
    {
      System.out.print("R");
    }
  }
}
```

1. The statement if(! isOld || y > z) returns false, because the first operand !isOld also returns false. In this case the block is ignored and R is not written to the standard output.
2. If z is equal to 17, the statement if(y > x && z > y && (x + 12) >= z) returns true. Because the first operand y > x is true, the second operand z > y is true and the third operand (x + 12) >= z also

returns true. The block is executed and P is written to the standard output.

If z is equal to 17, the statement if(x >= 6 || z <= y || z <= 18) returns true, because the operand z <= 18 returns true.

Quiz 7

```
class MyClass
{
  public static void main(String[] args)
  {
    int i1 = 3;
    int i2 = 5;
    int i3 = 12;
    int i4 = 20;

    i1 += 4;
    i2 *= 3;
    i3 /= 3;
    i4 -= 12;
    // Answer
    System.out.print("The answer is: ");
    i1++;
    i2 -= 3;
    i3 *= 2;
    i4 /= 4;

    System.out.print(i1 + ", ");
    System.out.print(i2 + ", ");
    System.out.print(i3 + ", ");
    System.out.print(i4 + " ");
  }
}
```

The result is that the code writes the following to the standard output.

The answer is: 8, 12, 8, 2

Quiz 8

```
class MyClass
{
  public static void main(String[] args)
  {
    int i1 = 22;
    int i2 = 17;
    int i3 = 30;

    i1 %= 6;
    i2 %= 5;
    i3 %= 6;

    // Answer
    System.out.print("The answer is: ");
    i1 %= 3;
    i2 %= 7;
    System.out.print(i1 + " ");
    System.out.print(i2 + " ");
    System.out.print(i3 + " ");
  }
```

```
}
```

The result is that the code writes the following to the standard output.

The answer is: 1 2 0

Quiz 9

```
class MyClass
{
  public static void main(String[] args)
  {
    int x = 6;
    int x2 = 4;
    int y = (x == 3) ? 24 : 8;
    int z = (x2 == 4) ? 33 : 21;

    System.out.print(y);
    System.out.print(z);
  }
}
```

The code writes 833 to the standard output.

4. Answers Conditional Statements

Quiz 1

```
class MyClass
{
  public static void main(String[] args)
  {
    int i = 2;
    // Answer
    if (i == 2)
    {
      System.out.print("N");
    }
    if (i > 0)
    {
      System.out.print("X");
      System.out.print("Y");
    }
    if (i > 3)
    {
      System.out.print("Z");
    }
  }
}
```

Quiz 2

```
class MyClass
{
  public static void main(String[] args)
  {
    int a = 3;
    int b = 1;
    int x = 0;

    if (a > b)
    {
      x++;
      if (a > x)
      {
        x += 5;
      }
      x -= 4;
    }
    if (b == a)
    {
      x += 2;
      if (x < b)
      {
        x += 3;
      }
    }
    System.out.print(x);
    // Answer
    if (a <= 4)
    {
      System.out.print("G");
    }
  }
}
```

Quiz 3

```
class MyClass
{
  public static void main(String[] args)
  {
    char c1 = 'g';
    char c2 = 'h';

    if (c1 == 'k')
    {
      System.out.print('w');
    }
    if (c2 == 'h')
    {
      System.out.print('x');
      System.out.print('p');
    }
    if (c1 != c2)
    {
      System.out.print('y');
    }
    // Answer
    if (c1 == 'd')
    {
      // ignored
    }
    else
    {
      System.out.print('z');
    }
  }
}
```

Quiz 4

```
class MyClass
{
  public static void main(String[] args)
  {
    int a = 2;
    int b = 2;
    int x = 5;

    // answer 1
    if (a != b)
    {
      x++;
    }
    // answer 2
    else if (b >= 1)
    {
      System.out.print("X");
    }
    else if (b == 2)
    {
      x += 2;
    }
    // wrong answer check out why
    /*
    else if(b >= 1) {
        System.out.print("X");
    }*/
    else
    {
      x += 3;
    }
```

```
      System.out.print(x);
   }
}
```

Quiz 5

```
class MyClass
{
   public static void main(String[] args)
   {
      int i = 1;
      int i2 = 4;
      int x = 2;

      if (i == (i2 - 3) && i2 > 5)
      {
         x++;
      }
      // answer
      else if ((i + i2) == 5)
      {
         System.out.print("D");
      }
      else if (i2 == 4)
      {
         x += 2;
      }
      // wrong answer, check out why
      /*else if((i + i2) == 5)
      {
         System.out.print("D");
      }*/
      else if (i2 > 3)
      {
         x += 3;
      }
      // wrong answer, check out why
      /*else if((i + i2) == 5)
      {
         System.out.print("D");
      }*/
      else
      {
         x += 4;
      }
      System.out.print(x);
   }
}
```

Quiz 6

```
class MyClass
{
   public static void main(String[] args)
   {
      int i1 = 3;
      int i2 = 9;
      int i3 = 12;
      int x = 0;

      if (x > -1)
      {
         x++;
         if (i3 == (i1 + i2))
         {
            x += 4;
            if (i1 < 5)
            {
               x += 2;
               // first possible answer
```

```
            System.out.print(x);
         }
         else if (i2 == 9)
         {
            x++;
         }
         else
         {
            x -= 2;
         }
         // second possible answer
         // system.out.print(x);
         x -= 6;
      }
      if (i3 < 10)
      {
         x += 7;
      }
      else
      {
         x += 5;
      }
      System.out.print(x);
   }
}
```

Quiz 7

```
class MyClass
{
   public static void main(String[] args)
   {
      int i = 2;
      int i2 = 5;
      int i3 = 9;
      int x = 3;
      boolean isSlow = true;

      if (isSlow)
      {
         x++;
         // answer
         System.out.print("x" + x + ", ");
         if (i >= 2 && i2 > 7)
         {
            x += 4;
            System.out.print("x" + x + ", ");
            if (i3 == 9)
            {
               x += 5;
               System.out.print("x" + x + ", ");
            }
         }
         else
         {
            x += 6;
            System.out.print("x" + x + ", ");
            if (i3 >= 3)
            {
               x += 7;
            }
            System.out.print("x" + x + ", ");
         }
         x += 3;
      }
      System.out.print("x" + x);
   }
}
```

```
}
```

Answer

The program writes "x4, x10, x17, x20" to the standard output.

Quiz 8

```
class MyClass
{
  public static void main(String[] args)
  {
    int x = 8;

    switch (x)
    {
      case 6:
        x += 5;
      case 7:
        x += 3;
      case 8:
        x += 2;
        // answer 2
        break;
      case 9:
        x++;
        // answer 1
        break;
      default:
        x += 4;
    }
    System.out.print(x);
  }
}
```

Answer

15

10

Quiz 9

```
class Year
{
  public static void main(String[] args)
  {
    int intMonth = 9;
    String strMonth;

    switch (intMonth)
    {
      case 1:
        strMonth = "JAN ";
        break;
      case 2:
        strMonth = "FEB ";
        break;
      case 3:
        strMonth = "MAR ";
        break;
      case 4:
        strMonth = "APR ";
        break;
      case 5:
        strMonth = "MAY ";
```

```
        break;
      case 6:
        strMonth = "JUN ";
        break;
      case 7:
        strMonth = "JUL ";
        break;
      case 8:
        strMonth = "AUG ";
        break;
      case 9:
        strMonth = "SEP ";
        break;
      case 10:
        strMonth = "OCT ";
        break;
      case 11:
        strMonth = "NOV ";
        break;
      case 12:
        strMonth = "DEC ";
        break;
      default:
        strMonth = "INVALID ";
    }
    System.out.println(strMonth);
  }
}
```

Quiz 10

```
class Examen
{
  public static void main(String args[])
  {
    // answer 3
    char grade = 'N';

    switch (grade)
    {
      case 'A':
        System.out.print("Excellent! ");
        break;
      case 'B':
        System.out.print("Very good ");
        break;
      // answer 1
      case 'C':
        System.out.print("Good ");
        break;
      // answer 2
      case 'D':
        System.out.print("Fair ");
        break;
      case 'E':
        System.out.print("Try again ");
        break;
      default:
        System.out.print("Invalid ");
    }
  }
}
```

5. Answers Iteration (Loop) Statements

Quiz 1

```java
class MyLoop
{
  public static void main(String[] args)
  {
    int i = 5;

    while (i > 1)
    {
      i--;
      System.out.print(i);
    }
  }
}
```

21

When i is equal to 1, nothing is written to the standard output because the condition i>1 is false.

when i is equal to 2 the answer is 1.

When i is equal to 5, the answer is 4321.

Quiz 2

```java
class MyLoop
{
  public static void main(String[] args)
  {
    int i = 8;

    while (i > 1)
    {
      i++;
      System.out.print(i);
      // answer
      // i -= 5;
    }
  }
}
```

The statement while(i > 1) returns always true, because i is equal to 8 and each time

the loop is executed the statement i ++; increments the value of i by one.

The value of i remains greater than one forever.

Quiz 3

```java
class MyLoop
{
  public static void main(String[] args)
  {
    int i = 4;

    do
    {
      i += 6;
      System.out.print(i);
    }
    while (i <= 12);
  }
}
```

The result is 1016.

Quiz 4

```java
class MyLoop
{
  public static void main(String[] args)
  {
    int i = 2;

    do
    {
      i += 3;
      if (i != 4)
      {
        System.out.print("x");
      }
      else
      {
        System.out.print("y");
      }
    }
    while (i < 10);
  }
}
```

The program loops endlessly, because the statement while(i != 10) always returns false.

The program writes xxx to the standard output.

Quiz 5

```java
class MyLoop
{
  public static void main(String[] args)
  {
    // answer
    for (int i = 1; i < 10; i += 3)
    {
      System.out.print(i);
    }
  }
}
```

The program writes 147 to the standard output.

Quiz 6

```java
class MyLoop
{
  public static void main(String[] args)
  {
    int x = 1;
    // answer
    for (int i = 3; i < 13; i += 5)
    {
      x += i;
```

```
    }
    x -= 2;
    System.out.print(x);
  }
}
```

The program writes 10 to the standard output.

Quiz 7

```
class MyLoop
{
  public static void main(String[] args)
  {
    char c = 'a';
    char c2 = 'b';
    // answer
    for (int i = 4; i >= 0; i--)
    {
      if (i < 2 || i == 4)
      {
        System.out.print(c2);
      }
      else
      {
        System.out.print(c);
      }
    }
  }
}
```

The program writes baabb to the standard
    output.

Quiz 8

```
class MyLoop
{
  public static void main(String[] args)
  {
    int x = 14;
    int y = 5;

    for (int i = 0; i < 10; i++)
    {
      x += 2;
      y += 5;
      if (x >= 21)
      {
        // break;
      }
    }
    System.out.print(y);
  }
}
```

The program writes 25 to the standard output.
If you remove the break statement from the
    above program, it writes 55 to the standard
    output.

Quiz 9

```
class LeapYear
{
  public static void main(String[] args)
  {
    for (int jaar = 2016; jaar <= 2040; jaar++)
    {
      if ((jaar % 4 == 0))
      {
        // continue;
      }
      System.out.print(jaar + " ");
    }
  }
}
```

If you remove the continue statement, the
    program writes all the years from 2016 to
    2040 to the standard output.

Quiz 10

```
class MiniTheater
{
  public static void main(String[] args)
  {
    for (int row = 1; row <= 5; row++)
    {
      for (int column = 1; column < 4; column++)
      {
        if (row == 1 || row == 3)
        {
          continue;
        }
        System.out.print(row + "," + column + "
");
      }
    }
  }
}
```

Quiz 11

```
class Theater
{
  public static void main(String[] args)
  {
    outer:for (int row = 1; row < 4; row++)
    {
      inner:for (int column = 1; column < 5;
  column++)
      {
        if (column == 2 && column == 3)
        {
          break inner;
        }
        System.out.print(row + "," + column + "
");
      }
    }
  }
}
```

The program writes 1,1 1,2 1,3 1,4 2,1 2,2 2,3 2,4
    3,1 3,2 3,3 3,4 to the standard output.

6. Answers Classes, Objects and Constructors

Quiz 1

```java
class Employee
{
  String name = "Anna";
  int age = 22;
  String phone;
  String city;

  public static void main(String[] args)
  {
    Employee em = new Employee();
    Employee em2 = new Employee();
    Employee employee = new Employee();

    employee.name = "Emma";
    employee.age = 25;
    employee.phone = "00233-786854";
    employee.city = "New York City";

    em.name = "John";
    em.age = 20;
    em.phone = "00383-384833";
    em.city = "London";

    System.out.println("-------- Employees -----
    ------");
    System.out.println("Name:          " +
    em.name);
    System.out.println("Age:           " +
    em.age);
    System.out.println("Phone:         " +
    em.phone);
    System.out.println("City:          " +
    em.city);
    System.out.println("------------------");
    System.out.println("Name:          " +
    employee.name);
    System.out.println("Age:           " +
    employee.age);
    System.out.println("Phone:         " +
    employee.phone);
    System.out.println("City:          " +
    employee.city);
  }
}
```

If the program is compiled and run, the following is written to the standard output.

```
-------- Employees ----------
Name:      John
Age:       20
Phone:     00383-384833
City:      London
------------------
Name:      Emma
Age:       25
Phone:     00233-786854
City:      New York City
```

Quiz 2

```java
class MyClass
{
  int x;
  int y = 7;

  public static void main(String[] args)
  {
    MyClass mc = new MyClass();

    mc.x = 5;
    mc.y = 8;

    MyClass mc2 = new MyClass();
    MyClass mc3 = mc;

    System.out.println(mc.x + ", " + mc2.x + ",
    " + mc3.y);
    // answer
    System.out.print("The answer is: ");
    MyClass myClass = new MyClass();
    myClass = mc3;
    System.out.println(myClass.x + ", " +
    myClass.y);
  }
}
```

Quiz 3

```java
class MyClass
{
  int x = 2;
  int y = 5;

  // no-argument constructor
  MyClass()
  {
    // answer 1
    this(6, 3);
  }
  // one-argument constructor
  MyClass(int x)
  {
    this.y = x;
  }
  // two-arguments constructor
  MyClass(int x, int y)
  {
    this.x = x;
    this.y = y;
  }
  public static void main(String[] args)
  {
    MyClass mc = new MyClass();
    MyClass mc2 = new MyClass(7);
    MyClass mc3 = new MyClass(9, 3);
    System.out.println(mc.y + ", " + mc2.y + ",
    " + mc3.x);
    // answer 2
    MyClass myObject = new MyClass();
    // answer 3
    System.out.print("The answer is: ");
    System.out.print("x = " + myObject.x + ",
    ");
    System.out.print("y = " + myObject.y);
```

```
    }
}
```

The answer is: x = 6, y = 3

Quiz 4

```
class Staff
{
  String name = "Ron";
  double salary = 400.0;

  Staff(String name)
  {
    this(name, 780.0);
  }
  Staff(String name, double salary)
  {
    this.name = name;
    this.salary = salary;
  }
  public static void main(String[] args)
  {
    Staff st = new Staff("Ben");
    System.out.println(st.name + ", " +
    st.salary);
    // answer 1
    Staff staffObject = new Staff("Mary",
    2000.55);
    // answer 2
    System.out.print("The answer is: ");
    System.out.print(staffObject.name + ", " +
    staffObject.salary);
  }
}
```

The answer is: Mary, 2000.55

Quiz 5

```
class MyClass
{
  int x = 3;
  int y = 5;
  // answer 1
  int z;

  MyClass()
  {
    this(4, 6);
  }
  MyClass(int x, int y)
  {
    this.y = y;
  }
  // answer 2
  MyClass(int x, int y, int z)
  {
    this.x = x;
    this.y = y;
    this.z = z;
  }
  public static void main(String[] args)
  {
    MyClass mc = new MyClass();
```

```
    MyClass mc2 = new MyClass(9, 7);
    System.out.println(mc.x + ", " + mc.y + ", "
    + mc2.x + ", " + mc2.y);
    // answer 3
    MyClass mc3 = new MyClass(7, 8, 9);
    // answer 4
    System.out.print("The answer is: ");
    System.out.print(mc3.x + ", " + mc3.y + ", "
    + mc3.z);
  }
}
```

The answer is: 7, 8, 9

Assignment: Create a class Employee twice

```
// the first method without constructors
class Employee
{
  String name;
  double salary = 2400.55;
  String country = "France";

  public static void main(String[] args)
  {
    Employee employee = new Employee();
    Employee employee2 = new Employee();
    employee.name = "Olivia";
    employee.salary = 3100.45;
    employee.country = "Canada";
    employee2.name = "James";
    System.out.println("-------- Employees -----
    ------");
    System.out.println("Name:          " +
    employee.name);
    System.out.println("Salary:       $ " +
    employee.salary);
    System.out.println("Country:       " +
    employee.country);
    System.out.println("----------------");
    System.out.println("Name:          " +
    employee2.name);
    System.out.println("Salary:       $ " +
    employee2.salary);
    System.out.println("Country:       " +
    employee2.country);
  }
}

// the second method using constructors
class Employee
{
  String name;
  double salary;
  String country;

  Employee(String name)
  {
    this.name = name;
    this.salary = 2400.55;
    this.country = "France";
  }
  Employee(String name, double salary, String
   country)
  {
```

```java
    this.name = name;
    this.salary = salary;
    this.country = country;
  }
  public static void main(String[] args)
  {
    Employee employee = new Employee("Olivia",
3100.45, "Canada");
    Employee employee2 = new Employee("James");
    System.out.println("-------- Employees -----
------");
    System.out.println("Name:            " +
employee.name);
    System.out.println("Salary:        $ " +
employee.salary);
    System.out.println("Country:          " +
employee.country);
    System.out.println("----------------");
    System.out.println("Name:            " +
employee2.name);
    System.out.println("Salary:        $ " +
employee2.salary);
    System.out.println("Country:          " +
employee2.country);
  }
}
```

7. Answers Methods

Quiz 1

```java
class PreciousMetal
{
    double ozGold = 1300.0; // the price of one
    ounce of gold
    double ozSilver = 20.0; // the price of one
    ounce of silver
    double ozPlatinum = 936; // the price of one
    ounce of platinum
    boolean isGold = true;

    double getMetalPrice(boolean isGold, int
    ounce)
    {
        if (isGold)
        {
            return ozGold * ounce;
        }
        else
        {
            return ozSilver * ounce;
        }
    }
    // answer 1
    double getPlatinumPrice(double ounce)
    {
        return ounce * ozPlatinum;
    }
    public static void main(String[] args)
    {
        PreciousMetal pm = new PreciousMetal();
        System.out.print(pm.getMetalPrice(false,
        4));
        System.out.print(", ");
        System.out.println(pm.getMetalPrice(true,
        2));
        // answer 2, 3
        System.out.println("5.5 oz: " + "$ " +
        pm.getPlatinumPrice(5.5));
        System.out.println("4.5 oz: " + "$ " +
        pm.getPlatinumPrice(4.5));
        System.out.println("6.0 oz: " + "$ " +
        pm.getPlatinumPrice(6.0));
    }
}
```

Quiz 2

```java
class Calculation
{
    int i = 5;
    int i2 = 3;

    int getResult()
    {
        i++;
        if (i <= i2)
        {
```

```java
            return i * i2;
        }
        else if ((i + i2) >= 9)
        {
            return i + i2 + 5;
        }
        return i * i2 + 3;
    }
    // answer 1
    int calculate(int x, int y)
    {
        return x * y;
    }
    public static void main(String[] args)
    {
        Calculation cal = new Calculation();
        System.out.println(cal.getResult());
        // answer 2
        System.out.println("The answer is: ");
        System.out.println("22 * 4  = " +
        cal.calculate(22, 4));
        // answer 3
        System.out.println("9 * 12  = " +
        cal.calculate(9, 12));
        System.out.println("41 * 11 = " +
        cal.calculate(41, 11));
    }
}
```

Quiz 3

```java
public class MyClass
{
    int i = 3;
    int i2 = 8;

    MyClass()
    {
        i += 4;
        i2 += 2;
    }
    void print()
    {
        int x = i + i2;
        System.out.print(x);
    }
    // answer 1
    double getNetSalary(double grossSalary, double
    taxRate)
    {
        double taxAmount = grossSalary * taxRate;
        double netSalary = grossSalary - taxAmount;
        return netSalary;
    }
    public static void main(String[] args)
    {
        MyClass mc = new MyClass();
        // mc.print();
        // answer 2
        System.out.println("Calculate net salary,
        tax rate = 20%: ");
        System.out.println("$ 3000 is $ " +
        mc.getNetSalary(3000, 0.20));
        System.out.println("$ 2400 is $ " +
        mc.getNetSalary(2400, 0.20));
        System.out.println("$ 1466 is $ " +
        mc.getNetSalary(1466, 0.20));
```

```java
    System.out.println("Calculate net salary,
  tax rate = 30%: ");
    System.out.println("$ 3000 is $ " +
  mc.getNetSalary(3000, 0.30));
    System.out.println("$ 2400 is $ " +
  mc.getNetSalary(2400, 0.30));
    System.out.println("$ 1466 is $ " +
  mc.getNetSalary(1466, 0.30));
  }
}
```

Quiz 4

```java
class MyClass
{
  int x = 2;

  void print()
  {
    for (int i = 0; i <= 3; i++)
    {
      if (i < 2)
      {
        x++;
      }
      else
      {
        x += 2;
      }
    }
    System.out.print(x);
  }
  // answer 1,2
  int getGreaterNumber(int x, int y)
  {
    if (x > y)
    {
      return x;
    }
    else if (y > x)
    {
      return y;
    }
    else
    {
      return -1;
    }
  }
  public static void main(String[] args)
  {
    MyClass mc = new MyClass();
    // answer 3
    System.out.println(mc.getGreaterNumber(57,
57));
    System.out.println(mc.getGreaterNumber(49,
22));
    System.out.println(mc.getGreaterNumber(7,
89));
    System.out.println(mc.getGreaterNumber(0, -
3));
  }
}
```

Quiz 5

```java
class Currency
{
  //dollar exchange rate
  double euro = 0.907; // $1 = € 0.907
  double britishPound = 0.762; // $1 = £ 0.762
  double swissFranc = 0.986; // $1 = 0.986 CHF
  double chineseYuan = 6.674; // $1 = ¥ 6.674
  double russianRuble = 64.459; // $ 1 = 64.459;
    RUB

  void convertToDollar(char valuta, int bedrag)
  {
    switch (valuta)
    {
      case ('e'):
        System.out.print(bedrag * euro);
        break;
      case ('p'):
        System.out.print(bedrag * britishPound);
        break;
      case ('f'):
        System.out.print(bedrag * swissFranc);
        break;
      case ('y'):
        System.out.print(bedrag * chineseYuan);
        break;
      case ('r'):
        System.out.print(bedrag * russianRuble);
        break;
      default:
        System.out.print("Invalid");
    }
  }
  // answer 1
  double convertEuroToChineseYuan(double
   amountEuro)
  {
    double chineseYuan = amountEuro * (6.674 /
  0.907);
    return chineseYuan;
  }
  public static void main(String[] args)
  {
    Currency cr = new Currency();
    // cr.convertToDollar('y',100);
    // answer 2, 3
    System.out.println("€ 100 = ¥ " +
  cr.convertEuroToChineseYuan(100));
    System.out.println("€ 220 = ¥ " +
  cr.convertEuroToChineseYuan(220));
    System.out.println("€ 300 = ¥ " +
  cr.convertEuroToChineseYuan(300));
    System.out.println("€ 2    = ¥ " +
  cr.convertEuroToChineseYuan(2));

  }
}
```

Quiz 6

```java
class MyClass
{
  void myMethod(int x, int y)
  {
    int z = 4;
    int i = 3;
    i++;
```

```
    if (x < y)
    {
      z += 4;
    }
    if (x * x > y)
    {
      z += 2;
    }
    else
    {
      z += 6;
    }
    z++;
    System.out.print(z);
  }
  // answer 1
  int getSmallestNumber(int w, int x, int y)
  {
    int smallest = 0;
    if (w < x && w < y)
    {
      smallest = w;
    }
    else if (x < w && x < y)
    {
      smallest = x;
    }
    else if (y < w && y < x)
    {
      smallest = y;
    }
    return smallest;
  }
  public static void main(String[] args)
  {
    MyClass mc = new MyClass();
    // mc.myMethod(3,9);
    // answer 2, 3
    System.out.println("Smallest is: " +
    mc.getSmallestNumber(78, 44, 33));
    System.out.println("Smallest is: " +
    mc.getSmallestNumber(-2, 3, 0));
    System.out.println("Smallest is: " +
    mc.getSmallestNumber(55, 23, 123));
    System.out.println("Smallest is: " +
    mc.getSmallestNumber(44, 44, 20));
    System.out.println("Smallest is: " +
    mc.getSmallestNumber(34, 34, 34));
    System.out.println("Smallest is: " +
    mc.getSmallestNumber(11, 11, 55));
  }
}
```

```
    return price / ozGold;
  }
  public static void main(String[] args)
  {
    Gold gd = new Gold();
    // answer 2
    System.out.println("$ 7150 = " +
    gd.getAmountOunceByPrice(7150));
    System.out.println("$ 1300 = " +
    gd.getAmountOunceByPrice(1300));
    System.out.println("$ 2600 = " +
    gd.getAmountOunceByPrice(2600));
    System.out.println("$ 5525 = " +
    gd.getAmountOunceByPrice(5525));
  }
}
```

Assignment: A method that calculates amount ounce of gold

```
class Gold
{
  double ozGold = 1300.00; // the price of an
  ounce of gold

  // answer 1

  double getAmountOunceByPrice(double price)
  {
```

8. Answers Strings and StringBuffers

Quiz 1

```
class Quote
{
  String strQuote = "The weak can never
  forgive";
  // answer 1
  String myStr = "I feel good";

  void myMethod()
  {
    System.out.print(strQuote.charAt(4));
    System.out.print(", " +
  strQuote.indexOf('k'));
    System.out.print(", " +
  strQuote.indexOf('e'));
  }
  public static void main(String[] args)
  {
    Quote qt = new Quote();
    // ms.myMethod();
    // answer 2
    System.out.print(qt.myStr.charAt(7));
    // answer 3
    System.out.print(", " +
  qt.myStr.indexOf('l'));
  }
}
```

If this program compiled and run it writes g, 5 to
the standard output.

Quiz 2

```
class MyClass
{
  String str1 = "Jack";
  String str2 = new String("Jack");

  void myMethod()
  {
    if (str1 == str2)
    {
      System.out.print("X");
    }
    if (str1.equals(str2))
    {
      System.out.print("Y");
    }
    else
    {
      System.out.print("Z");
    }
  }
  // Answer 1
  boolean compareTwoStrings(String s1, String
   s2)
  {
    return s1.equals(s2);
  }
  public static void main(String[] args)
  {
```

```
    MyClass mc = new MyClass();
    // mc.myMethod();
    // Answer 2

    System.out.println(mc.compareTwoStrings("Fran
    ce", "france"));
    // Answer 3

    System.out.println(mc.compareTwoStrings("Hell
    o", "Hello"));

    System.out.println(mc.compareTwoStrings("123S
    tr", "1234Str"));
     System.out.println(mc.compareTwoStrings("My
    friend", "My friend"));
  }
}
```

Quiz 3

```
class MyClass
{
  String strQuote = "We cannot solve our
  problems with the same " +
      "thinking we used when we created them.
  Albert Einstein";

  void myMethod()
  {
    System.out.println(strQuote.substring(21,
    26));
  }
  public static void main(String[] args)
  {
    MyClass mc = new MyClass();
    mc.myMethod();
    // answer 1
    System.out.print(mc.strQuote.substring(82,
    97));
  }
}
```

Quiz 4

```
class MyClass
{
  String str = "He$llo $World$";

  void myMethod()
  {
    System.out.print(str.replace("$", ""));
  }
  // answer 1
  String replaceEuroWithDollar(String str)
  {
    return str.replace("€", "$");
  }
  public static void main(String[] args)
  {
    MyClass mc = new MyClass();
    // mc.myMethod();
    // answer 2
    String str = mc.replaceEuroWithDollar("€
    233, € 12, € 90, € 62");
    System.out.print(str);
  }
```

```
}
```

Quiz 5

```java
class MyClass
{
  String str = " the subconscious mind ";

  void myMethod()
  {
    int strLength = str.length();
    str = str.toUpperCase();
    str = str.trim();
    System.out.print(strLength + " " + str + " "
  + str.length());
  }
  // Answer 1
  int getNrCharacter(String str)
  {
    return str.length(); // index starts from 0
  }
  public static void main(String[] args)
  {
   MyClass mc = new MyClass();
   // mc.myMethod();
   // Answer 2a
   int quote1 = mc.getNrCharacter("What we
  think, we become.");
   System.out.println("The first quote: " +
  quote1 + " characters");
   // Answer 2b
   int quote2 = mc.getNrCharacter("Logic will
  get you from A to B. " +
       "Imagination will take you everywhere");
   System.out.print("The second quote: " +
  quote2 + " characters");
  }
}
```

Quiz 6

```java
class MyClass
{
  StringBuffer sb = new StringBuffer();
  StringBuffer sb2 = new StringBuffer("Jack");

  void myMethod()
  {
    sb.append("Elvis ");
    sb2.append(" Ben");
    sb.append(22);
    // Answer 1
    sb.append(" music");
    // Answer 2
    sb2.append(" 2000");
    System.out.print(sb + ", " + sb2);
  }
  public static void main(String[] args)
  {
    MyClass mc = new MyClass();
    mc.myMethod();
  }
}
```

Quiz 7

```java
class MyClass
{
  StringBuffer sb = new StringBuffer("He is
  friend.");
  // answer 1
  StringBuffer sb2 = new StringBuffer("He is
  from ,,, India");

  void myMethod()
  {
    // insert code here
    System.out.print(sb);
  }
  public static void main(String[] args)
  {
    MyClass mc = new MyClass();
    // mc.myMethod();
    // answer 2
    System.out.print(mc.sb2.delete(11, 15));
  }
}
```

Quiz 8

```java
class MyClass
{
  StringBuffer sb = new StringBuffer("He was her
  friend");

  void myMethod()
  {
    // insert code here
    System.out.print(sb);
  }
  // answer 1
  String convertSbToString(StringBuffer sb)
  {
    return sb.toString();
  }
  public static void main(String[] args)
  {
    MyClass mc = new MyClass();
    // mc.myMethod();
    // answer 2
    String strSb = mc.convertSbToString(mc.sb);
    System.out.print(strSb);
  }
}
```

Assignment: Methods of the String class

```java
class TextManipulation
{
  void stringDemo()
  {
    String text = "Brazil $ is $ one $of the
    largest country in the $ world.";
    System.out.println("Upper case: " +
    text.toUpperCase());
    System.out.println("Lower case: " +
    text.toLowerCase());
    System.out.println("Number chars: " +
    text.length());
    System.out.println("Remove $: " +
    text.replace("$", ""));
```

```
  System.out.println("Remove first 14 chars: "
+ text.substring(14));
  System.out.println("Return only largest
country:" + text.substring(26, 41));
  System.out.println("The index of the first
$:" + text.indexOf("$"));
  System.out.println("The index of the Last
$:" + text.lastIndexOf("$"));
  System.out.println("Replace Brazil:" +
text.replace("Brazil", "Canada"));
}
public static void main(String[] args)
{

  TextManipulation tmObject = new
  TextManipulation();

  tmObject.stringDemo();

}

}
```

9. Answers Packages & access modifiers

Quiz 1

```java
public class ClassB
{
  public int w = 1;
  protected int x = 2;
  int y = 3;
  private int z = 4;
  // answer 1
  private char myChar;
}


public class ClassA
{
  public static void main(String[] args)
  {
    ClassB cb = new ClassB();
    // System.out.print(cb.w); /* 1 */
    // System.out.print(cb.x); /* 2 */
    // System.out.print(cb.y); /* 3 */
    // System.out.print(cb.z); /* 4 */
    // Answer 2
    // System.out.print(cb.myChar);
  }
}
```

Quiz 2

```java
package package_02;

public class ClassB
{
  public int w = 1;
  protected int x = 2;
  int y = 3;
  private int z = 4;
  // answer 1
  public int myInt;
}
package package_01;

import package_02.ClassB;

public class ClassA
{
  public static void main(String[] args)
  {
    ClassB cb = new ClassB();
    // System.out.print(cb.w); /* 1 */
    // System.out.print(cb.myInt);
    // System.out.print(cb.x); /* 2 */
    // System.out.print(cb.y); /* 3 */
    // System.out.print(cb.z); /* 4 */
    // answer 2
    System.out.print(cb.myInt);
  }
}
```

Quiz 3

ClassB becomes invisible, because the two classes namely; ClassA and ClassB are in two different packages.

Assignment: The classes Date and Student in different packages

```java
package assignment.calendar;

public class DateInfo
{
  private int day = 16;
  private int month = 3;
  private int year = 1998;

  public DateInfo(int day, int month, int year)
  {
    this.day = day;
    this.month = month;
    this.year = year;
  }
  public String getDateFormat()
  {
    return month + "-" + day + "-" + year;
  }
}
```

```java
package assignment.personal_data;

import assignment.calendar.DateInfo;

public class Student
{
  private String name;
  private DateInfo birthDate;

  public static void main(String[] args)
  {
    Student isab = new Student();
    Student dav = new Student();

    DateInfo bdIsab = new DateInfo(28, 8, 1998);
    DateInfo bdDav = new DateInfo(13, 9, 1996);

    isab.name = "Isabella";
    isab.birthDate = bdIsab;

    dav.name = "David";
    dav.birthDate = bdDav;

    System.out.println("---First Student---");
    System.out.println("Name: " + isab.name);
    System.out.println("Birth date: " +
    isab.birthDate.getDateFormat());
    System.out.println("---Second Student---");
    System.out.println("Name: " + dav.name);
    System.out.println("Birth date: " +
    dav.birthDate.getDateFormat());
  }
}
```

If this program is compiled and run, the
    following is written to the standard outpt.
---First Student---
Name: Isabella
Birth date: 8-28-1998
---Second Student---
Name: David
Birth date: 9-13-1996

10. Answers Array and ArrayList

Quiz 1

```java
public class MyArray
{
  public static void main(String[] args)
  {
    // answer
    int[] arrayInt = new int[11];
    for (int i = 0; i < arrayInt.length; i++)
    {
      System.out.print(arrayInt[i] + " ");
    }
  }
}
```

The number 11 in this case represents the length or the size of the arrayInt, and that is why the program prints 11 uninitialized integers to the standard output.

Quiz 2

```java
public class MyArray
{
  public static void main(String[] args)
  {
    int[] arr = new int[5];
    arr[0] = 3;
    arr[1] = 7;
    arr[4] = 3;
    arr[3] = 1;
    arr[1] = 8;

    for (int i = 0; i < arr.length; i++)
    {
      // answer 1
      if (arr[i] >= 3)
      {
        System.out.print(arr[i] + " ");
      }
    }
  }
}
```

Quiz 3

```java
import java.util.Arrays;

public class Animal
{
  public static void main(String[] args)
  {
    // answer 2
    String[] arrAnimal = new String[8];
    arrAnimal[0] = "Wolf ";
    arrAnimal[1] = "Lion ";
    arrAnimal[2] = "Leopard ";
    arrAnimal[3] = "Elephant ";
    arrAnimal[4] = "Tiger ";
    // answer 1
    arrAnimal[5] = "Bear ";
    arrAnimal[6] = "Zebra ";
    arrAnimal[7] = "Monkey ";
    // see the class "Arrays" of the Java
standard API

    Arrays.sort(arrAnimal);
    // answer 3
    for (int i = 0; i < arrAnimal.length; i++)
    {
      System.out.println(arrAnimal[i]);
    }
  }
}
```

2. The array size is 5, By adding three elements the error "java.lang.ArrayIndexOutOfBoundsException " is written to the standard output. To fix the error, you need to resize the array from 5 elements capacity to 8 elements.

Quiz 4

```java
import java.util.Arrays;

public class MyArray
{
  public static void main(String[] args)
  {
    char[] arrCharA = new char[4];
    arrCharA[0] = 'g';
    arrCharA[1] = 'h';
    arrCharA[2] = 'e';
    arrCharA[3] = 'f';
    // see the class "Arrays" of the Java
standard API
    char[] arrCharB = Arrays.copyOf(arrCharA,
arrCharA.length);
    Arrays.sort(arrCharA);
    // System.out.print(arrCharA[2]);
    // System.out.print(arrCharB[3]);
    // answer 1
    int[] arrayInt = new int[5];
    arrayInt[0] = 3;
    arrayInt[1] = 4;
    arrayInt[2] = 2;
    arrayInt[3] = 7;
    arrayInt[4] = 9;
    // answer 2
    for (int i = 0; i < arrayInt.length; i++)
    {
      System.out.println(arrayInt[i]);
    }
  }
}
```

Quiz 5

```java
import java.util.Arrays;

public class MyArray
{
```

```java
public static void main(String[] args)
{
  char[] arrCharA = new char[4];
  arrCharA[0] = 'w';
  arrCharA[1] = 'k';
  arrCharA[2] = 'd';
  arrCharA[3] = 'r';
  char[] arrCharB = arrCharA.clone();
  // returns the index of the element 'k'
  int i = Arrays.binarySearch(arrCharA, 'k');
  // checks whether the two arrays are equal
  boolean b = Arrays.equals(arrCharA,
  arrCharB);
  // System.out.print(i + " " + b);
  // Answer 1
  char[] arrayChar = new char[8];
  arrayChar[0] = 'R';
  arrayChar[1] = 'N';
  arrayChar[2] = 'B';
  arrayChar[3] = 'S';
  arrayChar[4] = 'M';
  arrayChar[5] = 'O';
  arrayChar[6] = 'A';
  arrayChar[7] = 'C';
  // Answer 2
  boolean isEqual = Arrays.equals(arrayChar,
  arrCharA);
  System.out.println("Is arrayChar equal to
  arrCharA? " + isEqual);
  // Answer 3
  Arrays.sort(arrayChar);
  // Answer 4
  for (int x = 0; x < arrayChar.length; x++)
  {
    System.out.print(arrayChar[x] + ", ");
  }
}
}
```

```java
  else
  {
    System.out.print("x3 ");
  }
}
}
public static void main(String[] args)
{
  MyClass mc = new MyClass();
  mc.myMethod();
}
}
```

This program writes the following to the standard output.
Is arrayChar equal to arrCharA? false
A, B, C, M, N, O, R, S,

Quiz 6

```java
public class MyClass
{
  void myMethod()
  {
    // Answer 1
    String strArray[] = { "n", "b", "a", "z" };
    for (int i = 0; i < strArray.length; i++)
    {
      if (strArray[i].equals("z"))
      {
        System.out.print("x1 ");
      }
      else if (strArray[i].equals("a"))
      {
        System.out.print("x2 ");
      }
      else if (strArray[i].equals("b"))
      {
        System.out.print("x2 ");
      }
```

Quiz 7

```java
import java.util.ArrayList;


public class CountryList

{

  public static void main(String[] args)

  {

    ArrayList<String> countries = new
    ArrayList<String>();

    countries.add("Germany");

    countries.add("United States");

    countries.add("Russia");

    countries.add("United Kingdom");

    countries.add(2, "India");

    System.out.println("");

    System.out.println("- Before removing
    Germany from the list -");


    for (int i = 0; i < countries.size(); i++)

    {

      System.out.print(" " + countries.get(i));

    }

    System.out.println("");

    System.out.println("");

    System.out.println("-------- Countries ----
    --");

    System.out.println("Is the list  empty: " +
    countries.isEmpty());

    System.out.println("Check Spain :       " +
    countries.contains("Spain"));

    System.out.println("Check Russia:       " +
    countries.contains("Russia"));

    System.out.println("Index US: " +
    countries.indexOf("United States"));

    System.out.println("The size:           " +
    countries.size());

    // Germany is the first country on the list,
    its index is 0

    countries.remove(0);

    System.out.println("");

    System.out.println("- After removing Germany
    from the list -");
```

```java
    for (int i = 0; i < countries.size(); i++)

    {

      System.out.print(" " + countries.get(i));

    }

  }

}
```

Quiz 8

```java
public class Student

{

  String name;

  int age;

  String email;


  public Student(String name, int age, String
   email)

  {

    this.name = name;

    this.age = age;

    this.email = email;

  }

}
```

```java
import java.util.ArrayList;


public class College

{

  private ArrayList<Student> studentList = new
  ArrayList<Student>();


  public void populateStudentArray()

  {

    Student st1 = new Student(" Smith", 24,
    "smith@itmail.com");

    Student st2 = new Student(" Jennifer", 22,
    "jennifer@dzork.com");

    Student st3 = new Student(" Thomas", 33,
    "thomas@ysmail.com");
```

```java
    Student st4 = new Student(" Susan", 25,
"susan@rzmail.com");

    Student st5 = new Student(" Rita", 28,
"rita@online.com");


    studentList.add(st1);

    studentList.add(st2);

    studentList.add(st3);

    studentList.add(st4);

    studentList.add(st5);

  }

  public static void main(String[] args)

  {

    College cl = new College();

    cl.populateStudentArray();


    for (int i = 0; i < cl.studentList.size();
i++)

    {


  System.out.print(cl.studentList.get(i).name +

        ", " + cl.studentList.get(i).age +

        ", " + cl.studentList.get(i).email);

    }

  }

}
```

Assignment: Add items to a shopping cart

```java
public class Item
{
  String name;

  double price;


  public Item(String name, double price)

  {

    this.name = name;

    this.price = price;
```

```java
    }

}


import java.util.ArrayList;


public class ShoppingCart

{

  // String[] shoppingCart = new String[4];

  private ArrayList<Item> items = new
   ArrayList<Item>();


  public void printItems()

  {

    for (int i = 0; i < items.size(); i++)

    {

      System.out.println("Item: " +
    items.get(i).name + ", Price: " +
    items.get(i).price);

    }

  }

  public static void main(String[] args)

  {

    Item item = new Item("Shirt", 20.39);

    Item item2 = new Item("Pants", 32.85);

    Item item3 = new Item("Socks", 11.25);

    Item item4 = new Item("Coat ", 120.65);


    ShoppingCart sc = new ShoppingCart();


    sc.items.add(item);

    sc.items.add(item2);

    sc.items.add(item3);

    sc.items.add(item4);


    sc.printItems();

  }

}
```

11. Answers Static members

Quiz 1

```java
public class Employee
{
  int nr; // instance variable
  static int stNr; // class variable

  public Employee()
  {
    nr++;
    stNr++;
  }
  public static void main(String[] args)
  {
    Employee emp1 = new Employee();
    Employee emp2 = new Employee();
    Employee emp3 = new Employee();
    // answer 1
    Employee emp4 = new Employee();
    Employee emp5 = new Employee();
    // answer 2, check the value of stNr
    System.out.print(Employee.stNr + ", ");
    System.out.print(emp1.nr + ", ");
    System.out.print(emp2.nr + ", ");
    System.out.print(emp3.nr);
  }
}
```

The program writes 5, 1, 1, 1 to the standard output.

Quiz 2

```java
public class MyClass
{
  static int x = 3;

  public MyClass()
  {
    x++;
  }
  public static int method(int i, int i2)
  {
    x += (i - i2);
    return x;
  }
  // answer 1
  public static void resetX(int resetNummer)
  {
    x = resetNummer;
  }
  public static void main(String[] args)
  {
    MyClass mk1 = new MyClass();
    MyClass mk2 = new MyClass();
    System.out.print(MyClass.x + ", ");
    MyClass mk3 = new MyClass();
    MyClass.method(8, 3);
    System.out.print(MyClass.x + ", ");
    // answer 2
    System.out.println("");
    MyClass.resetX(0);
    System.out.println(MyClass.x);
```

```java
    MyClass.resetX(10);
    System.out.println(MyClass.x);
    MyClass.resetX(100);
    System.out.println(MyClass.x);
  }
}
```

Quiz 3

```java
public class MyClass
{
  static int x = 6;
  int y = 3;

  MyClass()
  {
    x += 3;
    y += 2;
  }
  void method(int i)
  {
    this.y = y - i;
    x++;
  }
  public static void main(String[] args)
  {
    MyClass mc1 = new MyClass();
    MyClass mc2 = new MyClass();
    MyClass mc3 = new MyClass();
    mc1.method(3);
    // answer 1, 2, 3
    MyClass mc4, mc5, mc6, mc7, mc8;
    System.out.print(mc2.x + ", " + mc1.y);
  }
}
```

By creating object references the constructor is not called, therefore the value of the static variable x doesn't change.

Quiz 4

```java
public class MyClass
{
  static int x = 2;

  MyClass()
  {
    x++;
  }
  static void methodA(int i)
  {
    x = x - i;
  }
  int methodB(int i)
  {
    return x + i;
  }
  public static void main(String[] args)
  {
    MyClass mc1 = new MyClass();
    MyClass.methodA(2);
    MyClass mc2 = new MyClass();
    System.out.print(mc2.methodB(3));
  }
}
```

By replacing the statement x += 4 with the statement x++, the program writes 5 to the standard output. See the explanation of the quiz.

Quiz 5

```java
public class MyClass
{
  int x;
  StringBuffer sb = new StringBuffer();

  public MyClass()
  {
    myMethod();
  }
  public void myMethod()
  {
    x += 3;
    sb.append(x);
  }
  public static void main(String[] args)
  {
    MyClass mc = new MyClass();
    MyClass mc2 = new MyClass();
    MyClass mc3 = new MyClass();
    System.out.println(mc.sb);
  }
}
```

2. By removing the static keyword from the class variable x, the program writes 333 to the standard output.
4. By removing the both static keywords from the variables x and sb the program writes 3 to the standard output.
5. yes.

Assignment: Track the names of programming languages in a string

```java
public class ProgrammingLanguage
{
  static int numberOfLanguages;
  static String language = "";

  ProgrammingLanguage(String lg)
  {
    numberOfLanguages++;
    language += lg;
  }
  public static void main(String[] args)
  {
    ProgrammingLanguage pl1 = new
  ProgrammingLanguage("Java, ");
    ProgrammingLanguage pl2 = new
  ProgrammingLanguage("C++, ");
    ProgrammingLanguage pl3 = new
  ProgrammingLanguage("Python, ");
    ProgrammingLanguage pl4 = new
  ProgrammingLanguage("PHP, ");
    ProgrammingLanguage pl5 = new
  ProgrammingLanguage("Ruby");
    System.out.println("Nr: " +
  ProgrammingLanguage.numberOfLanguages);
    System.out.println("Languages: " +
  ProgrammingLanguage.language);
  }
}
```

The code writes the following to the standard output.

Nr: 5

Languages: Java, C++, Python, PHP, Ruby

12. Answers Inheritance

Quiz 1

```java
public class MySuper
{
  protected int x = 5;
}


public class MySub extends MySuper
{
  private int y = 8;

  MySub()
  {
    x += 2;
    y++;
    System.out.print(x + ", " + y);
  }
  public static void main(String[] args)
  {
    MySub ms = new MySub();
  }
}
```

The program writes 7, 9 to the standard output.

Quiz 2

```java
public class MySuper
{
  protected int x = 1;

  MySuper()
  {
    x += 2;
  }
}


public class MySub extends MySuper
{
  MySub(int y)
  {
    x += y;
  }
  public static void main(String[] args)
  {
    MySub ms = new MySub(4);
    MySub ms2 = new MySub(6);
    System.out.print(ms2.x);
  }
}
```

The program writes 9 to the standard output.

Quiz 3

```java
public class MySuper
{
  protected char c = 'G';

  MySuper()
  {
    System.out.print('Q');
  }
```

```java
  }
  void method()
  {
    System.out.print(c);
  }
}


class MySub extends MySuper
{
  char c2 = 'A';

  MySub()
  {
    this('N');
    System.out.print(c2);
  }
  MySub(char c)
  {
    System.out.print(c);
  }
  void method()
  {
    super.method();
    System.out.print(c2);
  }
  public static void main(String[] args)
  {
    MySub mySub = new MySub();
    mySub.method();
  }
}
```

By creating mySub object, the MySuper()
  constructor is called and it writes "Q" to the
  standard output.
The result is: QNAGA

Quiz 4

```java
public class SuperB
{
  protected int x = 3;

  public SuperB()
  {
    x += 2;
    System.out.print(" x" + x);
  }
}


public class SuperA extends SuperB
{
  int y = 7;

  public SuperA()
  {
    y++;
    System.out.print(" y" + y);
  }
}


public class MySub extends SuperA
{
  int x;
```

```java
  public MySub()
  {
    x += 2;
    y += 3;
    System.out.print(" x" + x);
    System.out.print(" y" + y);
  }
  public static void main(String[] args)
  {
    MySub mySub = new MySub();
  }
}
```

The result would be: x5 y8 x2 y11
All the values remain as they were except the x
 that is printed inside MySub constructor.
That is because MySub now has its own x
 variable.

Quiz 5

```java
public class MySuper
{
  protected int x = 2;

  int method(int i)
  {
    return x + i;
  }
}

public class MySub extends MySuper
{
  int method(int i, int i2)
  {
    return method(i) + x + i2;
  }
  public static void main(String[] args)
  {
    MySub mySub = new MySub();
    System.out.print(mySub.method(2, 8));
  }
}
```

This program writes 14 to the standard output.

Quiz 6

```java
public class MySuper
{
  protected int x = 3;
  protected char e = 'd';

  void myMethod()
  {
    x += 4;
    System.out.print(e);
    System.out.print(x);
  }
}

public class MySub extends MySuper
{
```

```java
  char e = 'p';

  void myMethod()
  {
    x++;
    System.out.print(e);
    super.myMethod();
    x += 2;
    System.out.print(x);
  }
  public static void main(String[] args)
  {
    MySub ms = new MySub();
    ms.myMethod();
  }
}
```

This program writes pd810 to the standard
 output.

Quiz 7

```java
public class MySuper
{
  MySuper(String name)
  {
    this(name, "d");
    System.out.print(name);
  }
  MySuper(String name, String name2)
  {
    System.out.print(name);
    System.out.print(name2);
  }
}

public class MySub extends MySuper
{
  MySub(String name)
  {
    super("s");
    System.out.print(name);
  }
  public static void main(String[] args)
  {
    MySub ms = new MySub("x");
  }
}
```

This program writes sdsx to the standard output.

Quiz 8

```java
package package_02;

public class MySuper
{
  public String str1 = "String 1";
  protected String str2 = "String 2";
  String str3 = "String 3";
  private String str4 = "String 4";
  // answer 1
  protected int myInt;
}
```

```java
package answer._12_inheritance.qz08.package_01;

import
  answer._12_inheritance.qz08.package_02.MySuper;

public class MySub extends MySuper
{
  public static void main(String[] args)
  {
    MySuper mySuper = new MySuper();
    MySub mySub = new MySub();
    // System.out.print(mySuper.str1); /* 1 */
    // System.out.print(mySuper.str2); /* 2 */
    // System.out.print(mySuper.str3); /* 3 */
    // System.out.print(mySuper.str4); /* 4 */
    // System.out.print(mySub.str2); /* 5 */
    // System.out.print(mySub.str1);
    // Answer 2, 3
    // System.out.print(mySuper.myInt); //
    mySuper cannot access myInt
    System.out.print(mySub.myInt); // mySub can
    access myInt
  }
}
```

Assignment: Inheritance and overriding methods

```java
public class Vehicle
{
  protected String brand;
  protected int manufactureYear;
  protected String color;

  public Vehicle(String brand, int
  manufactureYear, String color)
  {
    this.brand = brand;
    this.manufactureYear = manufactureYear;
    this.color = color;
  }
  public void print()
  {
    System.out.println("Brand:
    "+brand);
    System.out.println("Manufacture year:
    "+manufactureYear);
    System.out.println("Color:
    "+color);
  }
}

public class Car extends Vehicle
{
  private int maxNrPassenger;

  public Car(String brand, int manufactureYear,
  String color, int maxNrPassenger)
  {
    super(brand, manufactureYear, color);
    this.maxNrPassenger = maxNrPassenger;
  }
  public void print()
  {
    System.out.println("--Car---");
    super.print();
```

```java
    System.out.println("Max passengers: " +
    maxNrPassenger);
  }
}

public class Truck extends Vehicle
{
  private double maxLoad;

  public Truck(String brand, int
  manufactureYear, String color, double
  maxLoad)
  {
    super(brand, manufactureYear, color);
    this.maxLoad = maxLoad;
  }
  public void print()
  {
    System.out.println("---Truck---");
    super.print();
    System.out.println("Maximum Load:  " +
    maxLoad);
  }
}

public class TestProgram
{
  public static void main(String[] args)
  {
    Truck tk1 = new Truck("BMW", 2016, "green",
    6550);
    Truck tk2 = new Truck("Volvo", 2014,
    "black", 4000);

    Car car1 = new Car("Toyota", 2013, "red",
    5);
    Car car2 = new Car("Mazda", 2017, "blue",
    8);

    car1.print();
    car2.print();
    tk1.print();
    tk2.print();
  }
}
```

13. Answers Final classes and the final keyword

Quiz 1

Yes.
No, you cannot extend final classes.

Quiz 2

Although the method methodeB returns a variable type int, its name causes nevertheless, an error. The reason is that this method has the same number of parameters and the same variable type as the final method methodeB of the superclass.

Quiz 3

```java
public class MySuper
{
  final int x = 4;

  final String methodA(int i, String s)
  {
    String str = i + ", " + s;
    return str;
  }
}
public class MyClass extends MySuper
{
  int x = 3;

  String methodA(String s, int i)
  {
    String str = s + ", " + i;
    // super.x++;
    return str;
  }
  public static void main(String[] args)
  {
    MySuper ms = new MySuper();
    System.out.print(ms.methodA(23, "Emma"));
  }
}
```

The variable x in the superclass is final , so its value is not be changed . A final variable is actually a constant.

Quiz 4

```java
public class MySuper
{
  final void methodeA(int x, double y)
  {
    double z = x * y;
    System.out.print(z);
  }
```

```java
}

public final class MyClass extends MySuper
{
  void methodeA(int x, int y)
  {
    int z = x - y;
    System.out.print(z);
  }
  public static void main(String[] args)
  {
    MyClass mc = new MyClass();
    // mc.methodeA(5,3.0);
    mc.methodeA(6, 4);
  }
}
```

The program writes 2 to the standard output.

Assignment: How to use the class Math in the Java standard-API

You cannot extend the class Math.
The class Math is final therefore it is not possible to use it as a superclass for your class.
No, because all the methods of the class Math are static and you can invoke them by using the name of the class Math.

For the rest of the question see the code.

```java
public class MyCalculation
{
  public static void main(String[] args)
  {
    System.out.println("The greater number is:
" + Math.max(35, 46));
    System.out.println("The smaller number is:
" + Math.min(46.98, 44.99));
    System.out.println("The rootof 81 is:
" + Math.sqrt(81.0));
    System.out.println("The random number is:
" + Math.random());
  }
}
```

This code writes the following to the standard output.

The greater number is: 46
The smaller number is: 44.99
The rootof 81 is: 9.0
The random number is: 0.4192215620231091

14. Answers Abstract classes

Quiz 1

```java
public abstract class MyAbstract
{
  protected int x = 6;

  public MyAbstract()
  {
    x += 2;
  }
  abstract int getSum(int x);
  abstract void printMyName(String name);
}

public class MyClass extends MyAbstract
{
  int getSum()
  {
    return x + 5;
  }
  int getSum(int x)
  {
    return super.x + x;
  }
  void printMyName(String name)
  {
    System.out.print("Name: " + name);
  }
  public static void main(String[] args)
  {
    MyClass mc = new MyClass();
    System.out.println(mc.getSum(4));
    mc.printMyName("Emily");
  }
}
```

This program writes the name Emily to the standard output.

Quiz 2

By adding the statement super(10); above the statement System.out.print("p"); the program writes n10ps to the standard output. See the explanation of this quiz.

Quiz 3

The program writes NOL27 to the standard output, because the statement this.str += str; adds the letter O to the str variable which has the value N.

Quiz 4

```java
public abstract class MyClassB
{
  MyClassB()
  {
    System.out.print("a");
  }
  public abstract int getResult(int x, int y);
}

public class MyClassA extends MyClassB
{
  MyClassA()
  {
    System.out.print("b");
  }
  MyClassA(int i)
  {
    System.out.print("d" + i);
  }
  public int getResult(int x, int y)
  {
    return x * y;
  }
}

public class MyClass extends MyClassA
{
  MyClass(int i)
  {
    System.out.print("c" + i);
  }
  public static void main(String[] args)
  {
    new MyClass(4);
    new MyClassA(4);
  }
}
```

The class MyClassA extends the abstract class MyClassB, therfore it should override the abstract method getResult or the MyClassB should be declared abstract.

Quiz 5

```java
public abstract class MyAbstract
{
  int x;

  abstract void methodeA();
  abstract String methodeB(String s);
  // Methode 1
  public double getPrice(double price)
  {
    return price;
  }
  // Methode 2
  public static double getPrice2(double price)
  {
    return price;
  }
}

public class MyClass extends MyAbstract
{
  void methodeA()
```

```
  {
    System.out.print("x");
  }
  void methodeA(int x)
  {
    System.out.print("y" + x);
  }
  String methodeB(String s)
  {
    return s + x;
  }
  String methodeB(int x)
  {
    return "x" + x;
  }
  public static void main(String[] args)
  {
    MyClass mc = new MyClass();
    mc.methodeA();
    System.out.println(mc.methodeB("y"));
    // Methode 1
    System.out.println("The price is: " +
mc.getPrice(33));
    // Methode 2
    System.out.println("The price is: " +
MyAbstract.getPrice2(33));
  }
}
```

Answers

Yes.
By defining the method static, you can invoke
the method using the class name without the
necessity of instantiating any objects.

Assignment: What is the current date and time?

```
import java.util.Calendar;

public class DateAndTime
{
  public static void main(String[] args)
  {
    Calendar now = Calendar.getInstance();
    System.out.println(now.getTime());
  }
}
```

15. Answers Interfaces

Quiz 1

```java
public interface MyInterface
{
  int x = 5;

  void methode();
  void methode(int i);
}


public class MyClass implements MyInterface
{
  public void methode()
  {
    // x ++ ; /* 1*/
    System.out.print(x);
  }
  public void methode(int i)
  {
    int z = i;
    // z = z + x; /* 2*/
    methode();
    System.out.print(z);
  }
  public static void main(String[] args)
  {
    int x = 7;
    x++;
    new MyClass().methode(4);
  }
}
```

There would be no error because the statement x++; increments the value of the variable x inside the main method by one. This program writes 54 to the standard output.

Quiz 2

```java
public interface InterfaceA
{
  void myMethod();
  void myMethod(char c);
}

public interface InterfaceB
{
  int MAX_ALLOWED = 3;

  int getSum();
}

public class MyClass implements
InterfaceA,InterfaceB
{
  // int MAX_ALLOWED; /*1*/
  int z = 2;

  public void myMethod()
  {
```

```java
    z = MAX_ALLOWED + 4;
    System.out.print("H");
  }
  public void myMethod(char j)
  {
    // MAX_ALLOWED += 3; /* 2*/
    myMethod();
    System.out.print(j);
    System.out.print(z);
  }
  public int getSum()
  {
    return MAX_ALLOWED + z;
  }
  public static void main(String[] args)
  {
    MyClass mc = new MyClass();
    mc.myMethod();
  }
}
```

This code writes H to the standard output.

Quiz 3

An error occurs in the class MySuper, because it uses the variable x. Remember that MuSuper class has no access to the variable x of its subclass.
By executing the code, the output would be m4qw4.

Assignment: A practical application of interfaces

```java
public interface Payable
{
  double getSalary();
}

public class Employee implements Payable
{
  double taxRate = 0.30;
  double salary;

  public Employee(double salary)
  {
    this.salary = salary;
  }
  public double getSalary()
  {
    double netSalary = salary - (salary *
taxRate);
    return netSalary;
  }
}

public class Freelancer implements Payable
{
  int workingHours;
  double hourlyRate;
```

```java
  public Freelancer(int workingHours, double
hourlyRate)
  {
    this.workingHours = workingHours;
    this.hourlyRate = hourlyRate;
  }
  public double getSalary()
  {
    double salary = workingHours * hourlyRate;
    return salary;
  }
}

public class Test
{
  public static void main(String[] args)
  {
    Employee emp = new Employee(3000.0);
    Freelancer fr = new Freelancer(140, 60);
    System.out.println("The employee wage is:
$ " + emp.getSalary());
    System.out.println("The freelancer wage is:
$ " + fr.getSalary());
  }
}
```

This program writes the following to the standard output.

The employee wage is: $ 2100.0
The freelancer wage is: $ 8400.0

16. Answers Casting
Quiz 1

```java
public class MyClass
{
  public static void main(String[] args)
  {
    int i1 = 127;
    int i2 = 134;
    byte b1 = (byte) i1;
    byte b2 = (byte) i2;
    System.out.print(b1 + ", ");
    System.out.println(b2);
    // answer
    System.out.print("The answer is: ");
    int myInt = i1 + i2;
    System.out.print(myInt);
    // short myShort = i1;
  }
}
```

This program writes the following to the standard output.

127, -122
The answer is: 261

Quiz 2

```java
public class MyClass
{
  public static void main(String[] args)
  {
    int i = 122;
    i = 187; // answer
    double d = i;
    System.out.print(d);
  }
}
```

This program writes 187.0 to standard output.

Quiz 3

```java
public class MySuper
{
  protected int i = 5;

  public int method()
  {
    return 2 * i;
  }
}
public class MySub extends MySuper
{
  int i = 3;

  public int method()
  {
    return 2 * i;
  }
  public static void main(String[] args)
  {
```

```java
    MySuper s = new MySub();
    // Answer 1, 2
    MySub ms = (MySub) s;
    // Answer 3
    System.out.println(" " + ms.i + ", " +
ms.method());
    System.out.println(" " + s.i + ", " +
s.method());
  }
}
```

Quiz 4

```java
public class MySuper
{
  protected int x;

  MySuper()
  {
    x++;
    System.out.print("N");
  }
  int myMethod()
  {
    return x + 3;
  }
}
```

```java
public class MySub extends MySuper
{
  MySub()
  {
    x += 2;
    System.out.print("P");
  }
  int myMethod()
  {
    return x + 4;
  }
  public static void main(String[] args)
  {
    MySuper ms = new MySuper();
    System.out.print(ms.myMethod());
  }
}
```

The program writes N4 to the standard output.

Quiz 5

```java
public class MySuper
{
  public MySuper()
  {
    System.out.print("m");
  }
  public void method()
  {
    System.out.print("s");
  }
  public void method(int i)
  {
    method();
    System.out.print("k" + i);
  }
}
```

```java
public class MySub extends MySuper
{
  public void method()
  {
    System.out.print("t");
  }
  public static void main(String[] args)
  {
    // MySuper ms = new MySub();
    // Answer 1
    MySuper ms = new MySuper();
    ms.method(3);
  }
}
```

Assignment: Working with Java API documentation ArrayList

```java
import java.util.ArrayList;
import java.util.List;

public class MyList
{
  List<String> list = new ArrayList<String>();
  ArrayList<String> aList = new
ArrayList<String>();

  public static void main(String[] args)
  {
    MyList mc = new MyList();
    mc.aList.clone();
    mc.list.clone();
  }
}
```

The class ArrayList implements the interface
List. Therefore it must override all the methods
of the interface.
The class ArrayList also has its own specific
methods, which does not exist in the interface
List. One of those methods is the method clone.
Therefore, the object list cannot access the
method clone.

17. Answers Nested Classes

Quiz 1

```java
public class Outer
{
  int x;

  Outer()
  {
    x += 4;
  }

  class Inner
  {
    int y;

    public void methodA()
    {
      x++;
      System.out.print(x);
    }
  }

  public static void main(String[] args)
  {
    Outer.Inner inner = new Outer().new
Inner();
    inner.methodA();
  }
}
```

The output is 5, because the inner class has access to the integer variable x of the outer class.

Quiz 2

```java
public class Outer
{
  // answer
  private int a = 5;

  Outer()
  {
    a += 4;
  }

  class Inner
  {
    Inner()
    {
      a++;
    }
  }

  public static void main(String[] args)
  {
    Outer outer = new Outer();
    Inner inner = outer.new Inner();
    System.out.print(outer.a);
  }
}
```

This program writes 10 to the standard output.

Quiz 3

```java
class Outer
{
  private int x = 2;

  Outer()
  {
    this(3);
    x++;
  }
  Outer(int i)
  {
    x += i;
    System.out.print(x);
  }

  class Inner
  {
    public void methodA()
    {
      x -= 3;
      System.out.print(x);
    }
  }

  public static void main(String[] args)
  {
    // answer
    Outer.Inner inner = new Outer(7).new
Inner();
    inner.methodA();
  }
}
```

This program writes 96 to the standard output.

Quiz 4

```java
class Outer
{
  static int x = 3;

  Outer()
  {
    x += 4;
  }

  static class Nested
  {
    Nested()
    {
      x += 2;
    }
    int method(int i)
    {
      System.out.print(x);
      return i + x;
    }
  }

  public static void main(String[] args)
  {
    Outer outer = new Outer();
```

```
    Outer.Nested nested = new Outer.Nested();
    System.out.print(nested.method(2));
  }
}
```

By creating an instance of the Outer class the
no-argument Outer constructor is invoked.
x += 4; increments the value of x by 4.
x = 3 + 4 + 2 = 9.
The program writes 911 to the standard output.

Read the explanation of the quiz!

Assignment: Working with Java API documentation

```
public class Car
{
  String brand;
  String manufactureYear;
  String licensePlate;

  public Car(String brand, String
manufactureYear, String licensePlate)
  {
    this.brand = brand;
    this.manufactureYear = manufactureYear;
    this.licensePlate = licensePlate;
  }
  public void printInfo()
  {
    System.out.println("Brand:            "
+ brand);
    System.out.println("Year of manufacture: "
+ manufactureYear);
    System.out.println("License plate:      "
+ licensePlate);
  }

  public class Engine
  {
    String engineCode;
    String fuel;

    public Engine(String engineCode, String
fuel)
    {
      this.engineCode = engineCode;
      this.fuel = fuel;
    }
    public void printInfo()
    {
      System.out.println("Engine code:
" + engineCode);
      System.out.println("Fuel:
" + fuel);
    }
  }

  public static void main(String[] args)
  {
```

```
    Car car = new Car("BMW", "2016", "XN-45-
489");
    Engine engine = car.new Engine("N45B20A",
"Petrol");
    car.printInfo();
    engine.printInfo();
  }
}
```

18. Answers Exceptions

Quiz 1

```
public class MyClass
{
  public void method()
  {
    try
    {
      System.out.print("x");
      int x = Integer.parseInt("38");
      System.out.print("y");
    }
    catch (NumberFormatException e)
    {
      System.out.print("z");
    }
  }
  public static void main(String[] args)
  {
    MyClass mc = new MyClass();
    mc.method();
  }
}
```

3. The output is xy because we passed an int number to the method parseInt. That is what the program expects. The catch block is ignored.

Quiz 2

```
public class MyClass
{
  public void method()
  {
    try
    {
      int[] intArray = new int[5];
      int z = intArray[6];
      System.out.print("w");
    }
    catch (ArithmeticException e)
    {
      System.out.print("x");
    }
    catch (ArrayIndexOutOfBoundsException e)
    {
      System.out.print("y");
    }
  }
  public static void main(String[] args)
  {
    MyClass mc = new MyClass();
    mc.method();
  }
}
```

The finally-block is removed therefore z is not printed to the standard output.
The program writes only y to the standard output.

Quiz 3

```
public class MyClass
{
  String str = "Boris";

  public void method()
  {
    try
    {
      str.substring(1);
      System.out.print("s");
    }
    catch (NullPointerException e)
    {
      System.out.print("x");
    }
    catch (Exception e)
    {
      System.out.print("y");
    }
    finally
    {
      System.out.print("z");
    }
  }
  public static void main(String[] args)
  {
    MyClass mc = new MyClass();
    mc.method();
  }
}
```

The output of the program is "sz", because the str object is not null anymore.

Quiz 4

```
public class MyClass
{
  int x = 20;

  public void method()
  {
    try
    {
      int i = 2 / x;
      System.out.print("a");
    }
    catch (NullPointerException n)
    {
      System.out.print("b");
    }
    catch (ArithmeticException e)
    {
      System.out.print("d");
    }
    finally
    {
      System.out.print("f");
    }
  }
  public static void main(String[] args)
  {
    MyClass mc = new MyClass();
    mc.method();
```

```
    }
}
```

int i = 2/x was dividing a number by zero which
causes ArithmeticException.
By initializing the variable x, the divide isn't by zero
but by 20. In this case, the exception does not occur.
The try-catch is executed as well as the finally-block.
The program writes af to the standard output.

Quiz 5

```java
public class MyClass
{
  StringBuffer sb;
  int z;

  public void myMethod()
  {
    try
    {
      sb.append("s");
      z = 5 / 0;
    }
    catch (NullPointerException e)
    {
      System.out.print("n");
    }
    catch (ArithmeticException ae)
    {
      System.out.print("a");
    }
  }
  public static void main(String[] args)
  {
    MyClass mc = new MyClass();
    mc.myMethod();
  }
}
```

The first statement is sb.append("sb"); .
Since sb is only a reference to an object therefore, the
NullPointerException is caught.
The program writes n to the standard output.

Quiz 6

```java
public class MyClass
{
  static String str = "";

  static void calculate(int x, int y)
  {
    str += "A";
    if (y == 0)
    {
      throw new
ArrayIndexOutOfBoundsException();
    }
    int z = x / y;
    str += "B";
  }
```

```java
  public static void main(String[] args)
  {
    try
    {
      str += "C";
      calculate(10, 0);
      str += "D";
    }
    catch (ArithmeticException e)
    {
      str += "E";
    }
    catch (ArrayIndexOutOfBoundsException ae)
    {
      str += "F";
    }
    System.out.println(str);
  }
}
```

The code throws a wrong type of exception because
the exception has nothing to do with arrays. Anyway,
the catch block ArrayIndexOutOfBoundsException
is caught, and the program writes CAF to the
standard output.

Quiz 7

```java
public class MyClass
{
  public static void test(String str)
  {
    if (str == null)
    {
      throw new NullPointerException();
    }
    else
    {
      throw new RuntimeException();
    }
  }
  public static void main(String[] args)
  {
    try
    {
      System.out.print("A");
      test(null);
    }
    catch (NullPointerException e)
    {
      System.out.print("B");
    }
    catch (Exception e)
    {
      System.out.print("C");
    }
    finally
    {
      System.out.print("D");
    }
  }
}
```

The program writes ABD to the standard output, because the NullPointerException is thrown.import java.util.ArrayList;

Assignment: Create your own exception class

```java
public class MyException extends Exception
{
  public MyException(String message)
  {
    super(message);
  }
}
```

```java
import java.util.ArrayList;

public class Test
{
  private static ArrayList<String> movieList =
new ArrayList<String>();

  public static void populateList()
  {
    movieList.add("The Godfather");
    movieList.add("Titanic");
    movieList.add("Dances with Wolves");
    movieList.add("The Pianist");
    movieList.add("Wall Street");
    movieList.add("Amadeus");
  }
  public static String getMovie(int movieIndex)
throws MyException
  {
    if (movieIndex >= movieList.size())
    {
      throw new MyException("The movie " +
movieIndex + " does not exist.");
    }
    return movieList.get(movieIndex);
  }
  public static void main(String args[])
  {
    populateList();
    try
    {
      String movie = getMovie(15);
      System.out.print("The movie title is: " +
movie);
    }
    catch (MyException me)
    {
      System.out.print(me.getMessage());
      // me.printStackTrace();
    }
  }
}
```

Index

Made in the USA
Coppell, TX
04 June 2021